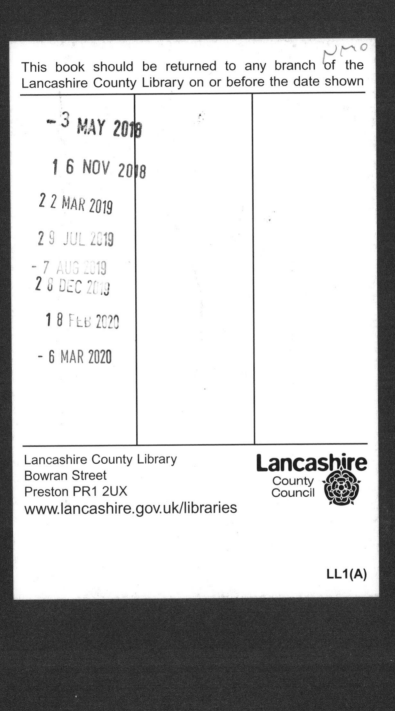

This book should be returned to any branch of the
Lancashire County Library on or before the date shown

ᴅᴍᴏ

- 3 MAY 2018

1 6 NOV 2018

2 2 MAR 2019

2 9 JUL 2019

- 7 AUG 2019
2 8 DEC 2019

1 8 FEB 2020

- 6 MAR 2020

Lancashire County Library
Bowran Street
Preston PR1 2UX
www.lancashire.gov.uk/libraries

Lancashire
County
Council

LL1(A)

LANCASHIRE COUNTY LIBRARY

30118133857197

D0236938

THE ULTIMATE UNOFFICIAL

ENCYCLOPEDIA

FOR

MINECRAFTERS

THE ULTIMATE UNOFFICIAL
ENCYCLOPEDIA
FOR
MINECRAFTERS

AN A-Z BOOK OF TIPS AND TRICKS

❮ MEGAN MILLER ❯

BLOOMSBURY

LONDON OXFORD NEW YORK NEW DELHI SYDNEY

This book is not authorized or sponsored by Mojang AB, Notch Development AB, or any other person or entity owning or controlling rights in the Minecraft name, trademark, or copyrights.

Lancashire Library Services	
30118133857197	
PETERS	J790MIL
£14.99	19-Jan-2017
NMO	

First published 2016 by Bloomsbury Publishing Plc

50 Bedford Square, London, WC1B 3DP

www.bloomsbury.com

Bloomsbury is a registered trademark of Bloomsbury Publishing Plc

Copyright © 2016 Bloomsbury Publishing Plc

Text copyright © 2016 Megan Miller

Minecraft® is a registered trademark of Notch Development AB.

The Minecraft game is copyright © Mojang AB.

The rights of Megan Miller to be identified as the author of this work respectively have been asserted by them in accordance with the Copyrights, Designs and Patents Act 1988.

ISBN 978-1-4088-8314-3

A CIP catalogue for this book is available from the British Library.

All rights reserved. No part of this publication may be reproduced in any form or by any means – graphic, electronic or mechanical, including photocopying, recording, taping or information storage and retrieval systems – without the prior permission in writing of the publishers.

All Internet addresses given in this book were correct at the time of going to press. The author and publishers regret any inconvenience caused if addresses have changed or if websites have ceased to exist, but can accept no responsibility for any such changes.

Printed in China by Leo Paper Products, Heshan, Guangdong

1 3 5 7 9 10 8 6 4 2

NOTE

The information provided in this book refers to features in the PC edition of Minecraft 1.9, the Combat Update. If you are using a different version, you may find some differences in gameplay. The Minecraft wiki at Minecraft.gamepedia.com is a great place to look for more information on the game. Also, if you are interested in playing with any of the mods, maps, or resource packs described, be sure to read all of the creator's instructions. Mod makers for Minecraft provide their mods for free, and they don't have the same support resources as a game manufacturer. That means they aren't able to update or address everybody's problems installing or working with a mod. It's pretty easy to mess up your version of Minecraft, and even your computer, when you download and install unofficial files, so make sure your current games are backed up.

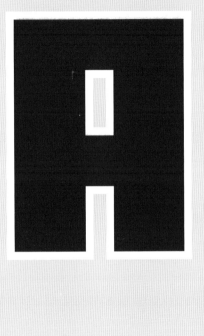

Abandoned mineshafts can be mazes of corridors, cobwebs, and fences reaching all directions. They are also a great source of loot.

ABANDONED MINESHAFTS

Abandoned mineshafts are generated randomly with each world, and you typically find them underground. The easiest way to find a mineshaft is to look in areas where they might be exposed, like ravines. Look for oak wood planks and torchlight to spot them. Also keep an eye out for them when you're travelling in the ocean. Parts of a mineshaft may be ex-

posed, and you can spot them by the torch-light.

Mineshafts actually generate with a "starting" point. This is a plain squareish room with a curved ceiling, a dirt floor, and exits often on all sides.

Mineshafts are a great source for rails, especially early on in a game when you may not have much iron. You can also find chests in minecarts that hold rare items. They may hold pumpkin or melon seeds, bread, coal, gold, iron, lapis, name tags, golden apples, torches and powered rails, detector rails and activator rails, and redstone. Rarely, you might even find more rails, horse armour and pickaxes, saddles, and even enchanted books or diamonds.

When you're in a mineshaft, be on the lookout for cave spiders. Mineshafts are the only places you'll find cave spiders. You'll probably hear them screeching before you see them, but also be on the lookout for the masses of cobwebs that signify a cave spider spawner.

Mineshafts can be incredibly big, especially if several mineshafts generate side by side, so have a plan for finding your way back out when you explore them.

ACHIEVEMENTS

Minecraft has a series of about thirty achievements; in console versions these may be called trophies. Achievements are a great way for a new player to start learning to play. Often you have to accomplish one achievement before you start another. The first is Taking Inventory, which you achieve by pressing E. In multiplayer, your achievement is shown in chat. You can find your achievements screen by opening up Options and choosing Achievements.

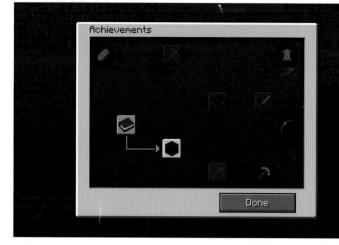

If you're new to Minecraft, building up achievements can be a great way to get started playing. Most random achievement? To achieve When Pigs Fly, you'll have to fly a pig off a cliff.

ANIMALS

Most animals in Minecraft are also called passive mobs, because they don't attack. (Wolves are neutral: they'll attack if they are attacked.) Almost all animals provide helpful drops when they are killed. For example, when a cow is killed, it drops beef. Different types of animal tend to spawn more in certain biomes. For example, you'll find more horses in open fields with grass. Don't kill all the animals in an area. They spawn rarely, so leave at least two so you can breed them.

Each animal also has its favourite food. You can feed two adult animals their favourite food to make them breed. You can feed a baby to make it grow up faster. If you hold the food in

Build a double-enclosure pen to stop animals that escape from their pen from getting any farther.

your hand, the animal will follow you. (They get distracted easily though, so you have to keep at it when you are leading them.)

When you design your animal pens, add in a second, exterior pen to work as a double gate system. If an animal escapes its pen through the gate, this will stop it from getting far. Also, for chicken pens, you will need to make a pen that is two blocks high, as chickens can jump over one-block fences.

ANVIL

You use anvils to enchant, repair, and name (or rename) weapons, tools, and armour. You name items by typing in the text box under Repair and Name in the anvil screen. This is the only way to assign a name for a name tag. Naming costs one experience level, plus more levels if you have worked on the item before.

You repair items by combining them with their base material. For example, you can repair an iron axe with iron ingots. You can enchant

Besides their practical uses, anvils can be a great decorative element, by themselves or stacked up together.

Arthropods, you must use the anvil to combine two items that each have a Level IV enchantment.

Each action you perform on the anvil costs experience levels. There are some complicated calculations that determine the experience cost. Basically, there are separate costs for renaming, repairing, and combining enchantments, as well as an increased cost if your item has been worked on previously. If the cost is more than thirty-nine levels, the anvil won't complete the repair and will give you the notice "Too Expensive!"

Enchanting with a book often costs less experience than combining two items. Anvils are better used for enchanted items usually, because repairing an unenchanted item can cost more than just replacing it. A really damaged diamond sword may take four diamonds to repair, when instead you can just make another sword with two diamonds and a stick.

Anvils are also one of the rare blocks in Minecraft that react to gravity (like sand and gravel), so they will fall if you place them over a block of air. They also cause damage: about two points of damage per block they have fallen, up to a maximum of forty points (twenty hearts). Anvils will last for about twenty-four repairs before they break and disappear with a loud clanging sound.

items with the anvil by combining an item with an enchanted book. This is the only way to get enchantments on a shear (Mending, Efficiency, Unbreaking). Use the anvil to enchant Elytra with Unbreaking and Mending. You can also combine similar items that are already enchanted (an enchanted diamond sword with another enchanted diamond sword, for example) to create one weapon or tool that has the enchantments from both of the first two items. (Tip! When you are combining two enchanted items, try them in both slots. The experience cost can be different depending on which one is the sacrifice item, in the slot furthest to the right.) Anvils are the only way to get some of the most powerful enchantments. For the strongest (Level V) enchantments for Efficiency, Power, Sharpness, Smite, Bane of

APPLES

Apples fall from oak and dark oak trees. Each oak or dark oak leaf block has a one in two hundred chance of dropping an apple, although you will get better odds if you use a tool with the Fortune enchantment.

Although apples theoretically only fall from oaks, you can still get them in a jungle. Jungle bushes are made from a single block of jungle wood and oak leaves. Because apples come from breaking leaf blocks, these jungle bushes can drop apples too (as well as oak saplings).

ARMOUR

In addition to protecting you from sword, arrow, and contact attacks damage, armour will protect you from falling anvils, cacti, chicken eggs, explosions, fire, fireballs from blazes or ghasts, fire charges, and lava. Without enchant-

Short jungle bushes are made from jungle wood *and* oak leaves, so they will also drop apples.

ments, armour does not protect you from other types of damage, like drowning or suffocating, falling, continued fire exposure, the Void, or potions. However, enchantments can add those protections.

To craft a full set of armour (boots, leggings, chestplate, and helmet), you'll need twenty-four pieces of the same material, either leather, gold, iron, or diamond. You can craft boots, a hel-met, and a chestplate very quickly by placing the material for all three on the crafting table in their usual positions. The material for the hel-met should be placed in the lower half of the crafting slots. Then you can press Shift and click three times to take out a chestplate, a helmet, and boots in that order.

Place your material like this in your craft-ing screen and shift-click three times to make a

The only way to get chainmail armour is to trade with villagers, or from rare drops by a skeleton or zombie wearing chainmail.

ARROWS

chestplate, a helmet, and boots fast.

Enchanted armour will protect you even more, although it has its limit. Some complicated maths involving a varying Enchantment Protection Factor, the level of enchantment, and a little randomization goes into exactly how many points of damage an enchanted suit will prevent. Armour durability is lowered when you receive damage by fighting, explosions, lava, or fire. When the durability of armour reaches zero, the durability bar disappears and you can use it only one more time.

Arrows travel through air or water from three to one hundred and twenty blocks, depending on the angle and the charge of the bow. After an object is hit, it will cool down for half a second before it can be hit again. Arrows can be tipped by crafting eight arrows around one bottle of potion. When a player or mob is hit with a tipped arrow, it takes on the effect of the potion but doesn't take on arrow damage.

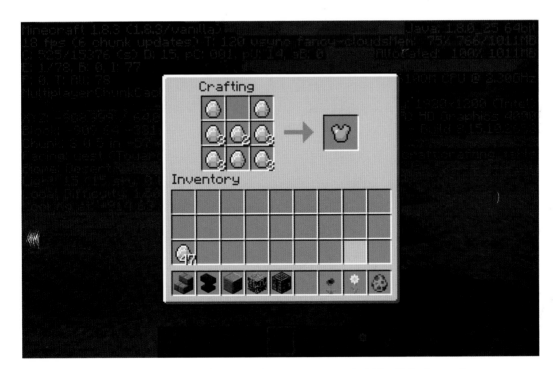

Place your material like this in your crafting screen and shift-click three times to make a chestplate, a helmet, and boots fast.

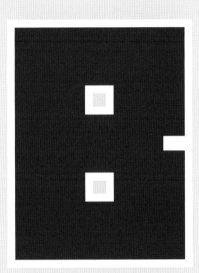

Adorable and deadly, baby zombies (and baby zombie villagers) won't burn up in sunlight and they are super fast.

BABY ZOMBIES

About 5 per cent of zombies spawn as babies. They are cute, fast, and can deal up to thirteen points of damage on Hard difficulty. Baby zombies are almost identical to regular size zombies, but they don't burn up in sunlight, they move faster, they make squeaky zombie noises, and they can fit through one-block holes. About 5 per cent of the rare baby zombies spawn as baby zombie villagers. (The baby zombie villager is easily distinguished by its villager unibrow.) Attack any type of baby zombie as fast as you can, or pillar up two blocks so they can't jump to get you but you can still reach them with your pointy sword.

Also, watch out for baby zombies on chickens. They're called chicken jockeys, and they run just as fast together. Because chickens can float slowly to the ground, they don't take fall damage. About 5 per cent of baby zombies spawn on chickens. In a chicken-populated area, this chance almost doubles. If you find a chicken wandering around a deep cave, chances are it once belonged to a baby zombie who happened to spawn there in the dark as a chicken jockey. The chicken somehow lost its rider. The baby zombie could have died, or if the pair came into flowing water, they would have separated.

BATS

If you hear a bat squeaking, you know that there is a cave nearby. Otherwise, bats are useless except for bow practice.

Bats sleep during the day, spawn at light Level 4 and below, and will fly straight into lava and burn up.

BEACONS

Beacons are blocks that give out light, like glowstone. If you activate them on a special pyramid, they emit columns of light into the sky and can give you special powers or status effects. They are one of the rarest Minecraft blocks, because you need a Nether star to build one. And to get a Nether star, you need to kill a Wither.

To activate a beacon, you must place it at the top of a pyramid of iron, gold, emerald, or diamond blocks. There are four sizes of pyramid you can build, and each one gives you a relative increase in range for its effects and more powers to choose from. The biggest pyramid has four levels, the bottom one being a 9x9-block square.

Once you've built your pyramid and placed your beacon, right-click it to open its interface. The left side shows you the primary powers, organized by the level of pyramid you need for that power. The right side shows you the secondary power, which is only available with a four-level pyramid. To activate a power, you first feed an ingot, diamond, or emerald (it doesn't matter which) into the slot at the bottom of the interface. Then choose your primary power (and secondary power, if available).

The primary powers you can choose from are Speed, Haste (for mining speed), Resistance (this improves your armour), Jump Boost, and

You can reuse the pyramid blocks from one beacon to create a new beacon to save a lot of material. You can also use dyed glass to change their beam colour.

Strength. The secondary power is either Regeneration or the option to boost your primary power to Level II. Finally, select the check mark to set the power. If you want to change the beacon's effects later, you'll need to feed it again. A one-level pyramid has a range of twenty blocks, and this goes up incrementally to a range of fifty blocks for a four-level pyramid.

When you are planning your beacon, place the pyramid as low underground as you can. Beacons will emit status effects downwards only to the level of range it has, but up to 256 blocks above. The beacon must have a clear opening to the sky. You can change the colour of the beacon's light by placing stained glass blocks or panes above it. You can even place different colours of glass above the first stained glass blocks to modify the first colour.

BEETROOT

If you have a beet in your hand, pigs will follow you wherever you lead them. Beets can also be used to craft beetroot soup and rose red dye. They can be farmed, traded, and harvested in villages.

It is very rare to find two biomes that are so different in temperature—a Jungle Biome and an Ice Plains Spikes Biome—next to each other!

BIOME

Minecraft has sixty-two different biomes or natural landscapes. Each biome type has different characteristics in terms of geography, plants, grass colour, leaf colour, animals, temperature, and weather. The game puts them into five categories (snowy, cold, medium/lush, dry/warm, and neutral) to help prevent opposite types of biomes being generated together, like desert and snow. The grass colour, leaf colour (except spruce and birch), and water colour in a biome depend on the biome's temperature and rainfall. Many of these biomes are variations of each other. There are Hills variations of many biomes, where you can anticipate running into hillier terrain. There are also M variations of many biomes. Many of the M biome variations are mountainous, while others have an unusual feature added to them. The M variations are rarer than their original biome.

Snowy biomes include Cold Beach, Cold Taiga, Frozen River, Ice Plains, and Ice Plains Spikes. It always snows in these biomes. If there are trees, they will usually be spruces. You'll

Super-tall birch trees generate in a Birch Forest M Biome.

find wolves in the warmer parts of snowy biomes, in the cold taiga areas.

Cold biomes include Extreme Hills, the warmer taiga biomes, and Stone Beach. Medium/lush biomes include Plains, Forest, Birch Forest, Roofed Forest, Flower Forest, Swampland, River, Beach, Jungle, and Mushroom Island. The dry/warm biomes include Desert, Savanna, Mesa, and Plateau. The neutral biomes include the Ocean and the Deep Ocean. The Void biome is a superflat world with no terrain at all, save for a stone platform at the spawn point.

BIRCH FOREST BIOME

The Birch Forest Biome is very similar to a regular Forest Biome, except all the trees are birch. As in a Forest Biome, you'll find flowers here, though not as many as in a Flower Forest Biome. As you might suspect, a Birch Forest Hills Biome has more hills. More interestingly, a Birch Forest M Biome has birch trees that are much, much taller than those in a regular Forest Biome or Birch Forest Biome. And in a Birch Forest Hills M Biome, you will have both the hills and the tall birch.

Nether fortresses have blaze spawners in special rooms exposed to the outside.

BLAZES

Blazes are hostile mobs found in Nether fortresses. Their bodies are grey smoke surrounded by three sections of rotating golden rods. When blazes see you, they rise up in the air, catch on fire, and then hurl three fireballs at you; and they'll do this over and over again. When you kill them, they drop blaze rods, which you need to make brewing stations, potions of Fire Resistance, and Eyes of Ender. Blazes can spawn randomly in a fortress, but a fortress also has one or more blaze spawn-

er rooms that have low walls and are reached by a short staircase. As long as you are not in Survival mode, you can mine a spawner with a pickaxe, and then you can use a spawner to

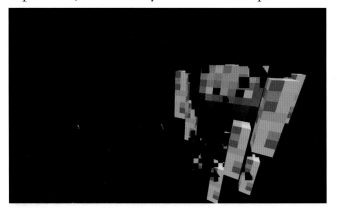

To fight blazes, use a Fire Resistance potion.

Right-click with a sword to block up to 50 per cent of incoming damage.

make a mob farm. If you don't want to use the spawner later, break it to stop it from spawning any more blazes.

To fight blazes, use Fire Resistance potions to protect yourself from their fireballs and rush them as they start to rise in the air. If you don't have potions (or golden apples) to help protect you against damage, wall the blazes off and attack them through a one-block hole. Blazes are also damaged by snowballs, so that is another way to attack them from a distance.

BLOCKING

Blocking is an essential technique in combat. You block attacks with a shield. Using a shield reduces incoming damage from a mob to 33 per cent, and completely prevents any damage from arrows, explosions and other non-mob items.

BLOCKS

Everything in Minecraft is made up of blocks. There are about 144 different types. Some are generated, others are created by natural events or combinations like snow and obsidian, and

Get away from land mobs in a boat. They'll only swim after you (and skeletons will shoot) for a short while.

others are part of structures like beds, doors, and chests. Each Minecraft block is defined as 1 metre cubed, or 3.3 feet in each direction. So if you want to build your own house in Minecraft, you can measure the walls in feet or metres and know about how many Minecraft blocks it will take.

BOATS

Boats are a great way to travel by sea quickly.

Simply use the directional keys to steer the boat forwards, backwards, left, or right. Boats are also a great way to get away from mobs at night if you are in a predicament and near water. A plus is that you won't lose hunger while you're in a boat.

BUILDING

It's very easy to lose track of where you are when you're counting, or miss a block, or even get interrupted and forget. One way to

Press Shift (sneak) and S to travel backward and place blocks, even over thin air!

keep track while you build is to use some kind of marker every fifth block. Then if you lose track, you can recount by fives to where you are. Build your houses so that their walls are an odd number of blocks long. That way, there will always be one block at the centre. This means you can place a single block item, like a door, in the centre. If you build with even numbers, there will be two blocks at the centre, so a single door or other single item can never be centred. To build out in front of you at a height, use the Shift key (or sneak key) with S to travel backwards and place one block at a time.

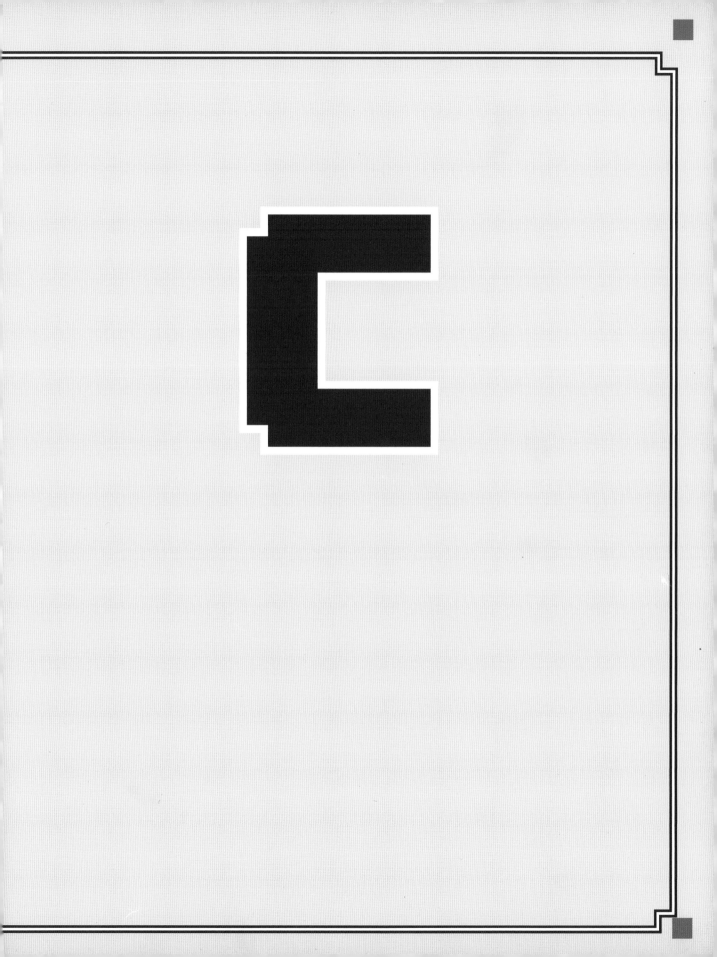

A simple automatic cactus farm, with blocks above the cacti. Cactus blocks pop off as the cacti grow, and water flows bring the cactus to hoppers attached to chests.

CACTUS

Cactus destroys objects thrown at it, so you can use it as a garbage can. Animals (and villagers) are easily damaged and killed by cactus, so be wary of it, however you can break it like any other block. You can't place cactus next to a block, and it will break if it tries to grow into a space with an adjacent block. You can use this feature to make a simple automatic cactus farm.

Just place a block above and to the left or right of the cactus. Use water to collect the broken drops and bring them to hoppers and chests. (A hopper will pull any items in the block above it and push them to any container with an inventory that the hopper is connected to. To connect a hopper to a chest or other container, press Shift and right-click the container with the hopper in your hand.)

CARROTS

To get carrots (and potatoes), you'll need to raid a village farm or wait for a rare drop from zombies. Neither carrots nor potatoes have seeds, so you just plant and replant them from your crop. Carrots are an essential ingredient in rabbit stew, and you also need carrots to breed pigs and rabbits.

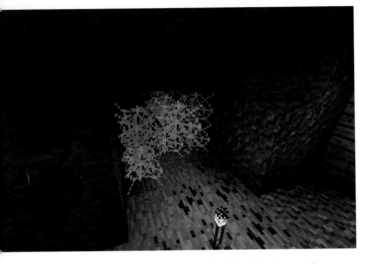

When you see the masses of cobwebs in an abandoned mineshaft, you know there is a poisonous cave spider nearby.

CAVE SPIDERS

Cave spiders are only found in abandoned mineshafts and they only spawn from a spawner. Their spawner is usually heavily guarded by masses of cobwebs, but you will probably hear them before you see the cobwebs. Cave spiders are faster and smaller than regular spiders and they are poisonous. Importantly, they can fit through a 1x1 block. Building a barricade with a 1x1 hole to attack them through won't quite work, but it can slow them down to coming through one at a time. If there are lots of spiders or you're by yourself, it's best to block off the spawning area first. Then you can tunnel below, above, or to the side of the corridor to get to the spawner and break it or disable it with torches.

CAVING

Caving can be a faster way of getting ores, because you don't have to dig out every block. But unless you are on Peaceful difficulty, you will still have to deal with hostile mobs spawning in the dark. A good tactic to minimize this is to run fast through the cave system in sections, lighting it up. To make sure you find your way back, use a system of placing torches only on the right or left and marking the way back when you get to a fork. Because torches on the wall don't light up quite as well as a torch in the middle of the floor, you can do both; place some torches on the right to mark the direction and some torches in the middle of the floor to light up as much as you can. Bring along a bucket of water when you cave (or mine), for turning lava to obsidian, and a stack of gravel for pillaring up and down. For extensive cave systems, choose a block or some other way to mark sections that you have explored and don't need to return to.

When you're caving, place one type of marker, like a torch on a dirt block, to show what's been explored. Place another type of marker, like two torches, to show you the right way back at a fork. And for a quick barrier, place blocks at eye level, leaving just one-block-high space above and below.

CHEATS

Although using cheats (or commands) can make playing Survival Minecraft less rewarding, they are very helpful in Creative mode. To use commands and cheats, you need to create your world with cheats enabled. To type a command, open up the chat window by pressing T. (You can also open up the chat window by typing the initial slash of the command.) You type your command into the chat window, preceded by a slash. For a list of available commands, type **/help**. You can show additional pages of this list by typing the page number, as in **/help 2**. For help with a spe-

For a list of commands, type **/help**, or **/help** followed by the page number, as in **/help 2**.

cific command, type **/help [command]**, where [command] is the name of the command. An example is **/help gamemode**.

Helpful commands to use in single-player Creative are:

- Switch to creative: **/gamemode c**
- Switch to survival: **/gamemode s**
- Change the difficulty level: **/difficulty 0** (for Peaceful) to **/difficulty 3** (Hard)
- Teleport to specific coordinates: **/tp X Y Z** (where X, Y, and Z are the coordinates)
- Stop it raining or snowing: **/toggledownfall**
- Die, to get back to spawn: **/kill**
- Change night to day: **/time set day**
- Change day to night: **/time set night**

If you didn't start your world with cheats on, and need to be able to use a command, you can play in LAN mode. To do this, while you're in the world, press Escape to go the Game Menu and then click the Open to LAN mode. (This allows other players on your home network to play in the same world as you.) Then, in the LAN world settings for other players screen (this will work for you too), select Allow Cheats or Creative Mode. This only lasts for as long as you are currently playing the world, though, and won't turn cheats on for playing in regular mode. Then click Start LAN World.

Chicks spawned by breaking an egg will still follow an adult chicken mother around.

CHICKENS

You can breed and lead chickens with wheat seeds. Chicks take twenty minutes to reach adulthood, but feeding them seeds will shorten that time by 10 per cent with each feeding.

When you throw a chicken egg, there is a one in eight chance it will spawn a chick. There is a tiny chance (one in 256) that it will spawn four chicks. If you throw the egg at a wall, the chick might suffocate in the wall. If you throw an egg at a mob, you can knock the mob back but not damage it. Chickens can be led or bred using wheat, beetroot, pumpkin, and melon seeds.

COBWEBS

When traveling through igloo basements, mineshafts, and stronghold libraries, cobwebs will slow you down, but they will also minimize fall damage. Using a sword, a piston, or water to get rid of cobwebs will drop one string, but shears, hands, or anything else will simply destroy the cobweb. You can use cobwebs in traps to slow mobs down or as decoration for haunted houses and chimney smoke.

COCOA BEANS

Cocoa beans, which you use for dye or chocolate chip cookies, grow on jungle trees, and breaking a cocoa pod gives you a group of beans. To grow them yourself, you must place them on jungle wood (it doesn't have to be a growing tree).

COMBAT

There are many ways to fight mobs, and developing new fighting techniques is one of the biggest challenges of Minecraft. Combine timing attacks, mastering shield use, using inventory wisely, honing your swordplay, and concocting potions, to level up your combat skills.

COMMAND BLOCKS

Command blocks are special Minecraft blocks you can use to execute special commands (to perform special actions) or cheats. For example, you can program a command block to give the player nearest to the block an enchanted diamond sword. There are hundreds of these commands in Minecraft. You right-click a command block to open the command screen and type in the command you want it to execute. You click a configured command block, or activate it, with a redstone signal, to execute the command. Command blocks are used for programming special events in adventure maps or multiplayer servers. For example, you could program command blocks to give new players in a world a special starter kit of a sword, axe, and three loaves of bread. Command blocks aren't available in Survival or in your Creative inventory. However, if you have cheats on, you can give them to yourself using the command /give <player> command_block <amount>. Substitute <player> with your username and <amount> with the number of blocks you want.

A command block is a special block you can use to execute special actions or programs within Minecraft.

You can do some crazy stuff with command blocks, like create a stack of mobs riding each other.

COOLDOWN TIMER

Each weapon has a cooldown timer that lets you time your attacks for maximum power. Spamming, or repeatedly clicking your sword to release a constant stream of attacks, creates a

The explosion from a charged creeper is more powerful than TNT and twice as strong as a regular creeper.

weak attack, while waiting until the cooldown timer has filled will cause more damage. The rarer the weapon (diamond versus wood), the faster it will recharge.

CREATIVE MODE

Creative mode allows you to fly around your world. You won't get hungry, or take damage if you fall, and mobs won't attack you. Because you can fly and are free from mobs, Creative mode is perfect for building or figuring out a complicated redstone contraption. You can play in Creative mode just to be free from mobs, survival, and hunger. This mode also gives you access to Minecraft blocks that aren't available in Survival mode or are difficult to get. For example, you can get spawn eggs (eggs you click to spawn a specific mob) and music discs. In Creative mode you can destroy blocks with your hand or any other item except a sword.

CREEPERS

Situational awareness is the best way to deal with creepers. Be on the lookout for them! They are so silent you will usually not hear their soft leafy footsteps until just before they start to detonate. If you hear that hiss, start running. You do have about one and a half seconds to get about five blocks away. If you succeed, the creeper will stop detonating, but it will still be after you! If you can't get far enough away to use a bow, sprint up to it to hit and knock it back with your sword, then press S to move back quickly. Do this again until you've killed it. Creepers are scared of ocelots and cats (tamed ocelots), and they will run away if they see them. They are not foolproof deterrents though—if you have a cat with you, you still need to be on the lookout.

If you see a creeper with a bluish glow around it, just run. This is a charged creeper that has been hit by lightning and its explosion is twice as powerful. If a charged creeper's explosion kills any skeletons, zombies, or other creepers, that mob will drop its head when it dies. Mob heads are mostly decorative. You can use a creeper head in banners to make a creeper face design. A Wither skeleton skull puts a skull and crossbones on a banner. In crafting fire-

When you deliver a critical hit, stars appear over your victim.

works, you can also use a creeper head to give the firework a creeper face shape. The head of a creeper, skeleton, or zombie can also be used as a disguise to give you a better chance of sneaking past other hostile mobs undetected.

CRITICAL HITS

Critical hits are a great fighting technique that delivers 50 per cent more damage to your foe. You make a critical hit when you jump (by yourself or off a block) and deliver your blow as you fall. Stars float over your opponent when you've made a critical hit. With a bow and arrow, you can deliver a critical hit by pulling your arrow fully back until your bow starts to shake a little.

When a player or mob receives damage, they turn red for a split second. During that short time, they are immune from taking more damage.

DAMAGE

When you strike a mob or player, you deal a specific amount of damage to it, depending on what you use to strike. Each damage point takes away one health point. Besides fighting, other things that can cause damage to a mob or player include cactus, drowning, explosions, falling, fire, lava, lightning, poison, suffocating, starvation, the Thorns enchantment on another player's armour, being in the Void, and the Wither effect. You can increase the amount of damage by up to 50 per cent by using a critical hit. A player or mob flashes red for half a second as it takes damage. During this half-second, the mob or player is immune to more damage. If you spam or repeatedly click your sword to do damage, some of those hits won't count.

If you need to do damage and you don't have a sword or bow, then axes, pickaxes, and shovels can also deal more damage than your fists. The amount of damage they do depends on their material and their attack strength. Diamond weapons and tools with a full attack strength bar after cooldown do the most damage.

DEATH

When your player dies, a death message is displayed telling how it happened. Some of these messages can be pretty funny, which may almost make up for the fact that you'll have to respawn and gather your goods all over again. Unless you are playing in Hardcore mode, you may often be dying and respawning back at your spawn point; it's part of the game. When you die, you lose all your experience, and your inventory and armour drop from you and hover around your death point. Your goods (and some experience

points) will stay there for about five minutes before despawning. This means you have a chance to get it all back, as long as you know where you died. If you died more than five minutes away from your spawn point, hope is still not lost. The chunk of the map you were in may have unloaded from computer memory (if there are no other players there), keeping your items as they were. The chunk will reload only when you get close, and by that time you may be able to get to your possessions before the five minutes are up. (Of course, if your inventory items drop onto cactus or into fire or lava when you die, they will be destroyed.)

DEBUG SCREEN

You can get some good information from the debug screen, which you open by pressing F3. It will show you a variety of data about chunk loading and entities, as well as your coordinates on the map (XYZ), what way you are facing (Facing), what biome you are in (Biome), and the light level of the block you're standing on (Light). Chunks describe the areas of a Minecraft world that are used in programming. They are sixteen blocks square and 256 blocks high (the full height of the game world). Entities are also a programming reference to certain types of moving game objects: these

After you die, you have about five minutes to get back to the scene of death to get your possessions.

are players and mobs, and other moving objects like minecarts, boats, and projectiles. The more chunks and entities that are loaded into computer memory, the more memory is taken up. For slower computers, this can mean a performance lag.

DEFENSIVE BUILDING

Probably the best defense against hostile mobs spawning near your home is to light up the area. Creepers, Endermen, skeletons, spiders, and zombies don't spawn in light levels above seven. Check your debug screen to see the light level of every block, and don't forget your roof! Next best are walls and fences. A two-block-high wall with an additional top lip or glass block layer to stop spiders from climbing up and over is very effective. Keep an eye out though for trees or hills that might allow mobs to jump over the wall. If you are playing in Hard difficulty, you'll also need an iron front door to stop zombies from breaking in.

DESERT BIOME

Along with sand, you can find villages, cactus, dead bushes, sugar cane (if the desert is close to a river or the ocean), and sandstone in a Desert Biome. It never rains in the desert. You can

A mysterious desert well has no known purpose.

The Desert M Biome variant is just like a Desert Biome, except for its shallow pools of water.

be in a neighbouring biome and if it rains, step one block over the border to the Desert Biome and the rain will stop. Rabbits are the only passive mobs that spawn in the desert. Rabbits can spawn on sand, but all other passive mobs spawn on grass, and there is no grass in the desert. This biome is the only place you'll find a desert temple or a desert well. Desert wells are square structures that look like village wells. There's no particular purpose to them except as landscape decoration.

If a dungeon spawns near the surface in a desert, you can often see the sand above it has fallen into a square shape. While you're travelling in a desert, look out for odd formations in the sand that may indicate a dungeon (with a mob spawner and chests of loot) is beneath. A modification of the Desert Biome is Desert M Biome, which has ponds. You can also find the Desert Hills Biome, a hillier version of the Desert Biome.

DESERT TEMPLES

Desert temples are a good source for rare loot you can't find anywhere else and a chance for finding valuable goods. You can find iron, gold, emeralds, diamonds, horse armour, saddles, and enchanted books in a desert temple. Of course, you may only find rotten flesh and bones. Desert temples are generated so that their entrance is at y=64. This means that they may often be partly or mostly buried in sand.

Inside the entrance is a pattern of orange and blue clay. This hides a very deep chamber that has a pressure plate connected to nine TNT blocks beneath its floor. Along the walls

An easy way to get down to defuse the TNT and get the treasure is to staircase down around the walls. You can also dig straight down and use the blocks to pillar back up.

are four chests that contain the loot. The easiest way to get down is to staircase down (dig out a staircase) around the walls. (You can also be safe digging straight down, and then use the sandstone you dug to pillar back up.) Once you're at the bottom of the chamber, use a pickaxe to break the pressure plate. You'll probably want to pick up the nine TNT blocks for yourself as well!

DIFFICULTY

There are four difficulty levels to choose from in Minecraft. In Peaceful difficulty (Level 0), no hostile mobs spawn and you have no hunger loss. You can still be killed by damage. If you switch to Peaceful from another difficulty, hostile mobs

Difficulty can be affected by the moon. During a full moon, slimes are more likely to spawn.

control this, because it is based on your gameplay difficulty level, how long your current chunk has been loaded, how long you've played in the world, and the phase of the moon. The higher the regional difficulty, the harder the gameplay actually is. Overall, the higher the gameplay difficulty level, the higher the regional difficulty level, and the closer the moon is to being a full moon, the more likely that:

- Explosions deal more damage
- Mobs spawn with armour, weapons, and enchanted armour and weapons
- Slimes are big
- Slimes spawn in swampland
- Spiders have status effects
- Villagers can be turned to zombies
- Zombies and skeletons pick up dropped items
- Zombies will seek you over a longer distance
- Zombies will break down wooden doors
- Zombies are able to call other zombies in for reinforcement
- Zombie pigmen spawn by portals in the Overworld.

(except for hostile wolves and shulkers) will disappear. Of the neutral mobs, only wolves will spawn in Peaceful. In Easy difficulty, hostile mobs give you minimal damage and your hunger can deplete and cause enough damage to leave you with five hearts. Cave spiders can't poison you and the Wither can't wither you.

In Normal difficulty, hostile mobs deal more damage. Hunger damage can leave you with as little as half of a heart, but you still won't die of starvation. In Hard difficulty, hostile mobs cause even more damage and you can die of starvation. Zombies can break down wooden doors and spiders can spawn with special powers, or status effects, like Invisibility and Speed.

In addition to the gameplay setting, there is also a regional difficulty level that works on Normal and Hard difficulty levels. You can't

You can equip a donkey with a saddle and a chest, although they can't wear armour.

DONKEYS

In Minecraft, donkeys are a type of horse. They behave the same way as regular horses, except they are smaller, have a greyish brown coat, and have longer ears. They can't wear armour, but you can equip them with a chest to carry your stuff around. Donkeys are slower and can't jump as high as regular horses, but you can feed, breed, and heal them in the same way as regular horses.

DURABILITY

Durability describes how long a weapon, tool, or piece of armour will last before it breaks. The durability of a weapon or tool depends on what type of item it is and its material. For armour, durability decreases the more damage it takes (and protects you from). An iron axe has a durability of 251, which means you can use it 251 times. Diamond is the most durable material, followed by iron, then chainmail for weapons, then gold and wood. When a weapon or tool breaks, it makes a clanking sound and disappears from your inventory. If you use a tool or weapon to do something it isn't meant for, like using a sword to break a dirt block, it usually counts as two uses, rather than one. So it's important to try to use the right tool for the job.

An item's durability bar only shows up when you have used the weapon or tool once. It starts off full and green and shortens and turns red as durability decreases. You can find the exact durability remaining on any tool or weapon in your inventory by pressing down the F3 and H buttons at the same time. When you hold your mouse over a weapon or tool in your inventory, a tooltip will say the exact durability left on the item.

DYES

There are sixteen dyes in Minecraft that you can use to colour banners, the beam of light from a beacon, glass blocks and panes, hardened clay, leather armour, sheep, and wool. Many dyes are made by simply placing items in a crafting screen: rose red (rose or beetroot), orange (orange tulip), dandelion yellow (dandelion), light blue (orchid), magenta (lilac, allium), pink (pink tulip, peony), light grey (white tulip, oxeye daisy, azure bluet). For cactus green, smelt (cook) a cactus in a furnace; for lapis lazuli (a deep blue dye), craft with the lapis lazuli ore; for white, craft with bone meal made from skeleton bones. Squid ink sacs make black, and cocoa beans make brown.

Dyes can also be made by mixing substances together. Lime is crafted from cactus green and bone meal mixed together; grey from bone meal and ink sac; cyan from cactus green and lapis lazuli; and purple from lapis lazuli and red dye.

You can also craft orange, magenta, light blue, and light grey if you don't have their relevant flowers, by mixing dyes. Orange is made from red and yellow, magenta from purple and blue, light blue from blue and white, and light grey from grey and white.

If you need a lot of dyed wool for a project, dye at least two sheep with the colour you want and breed them. That way you only have to use dye for the first sheep, as the lambs born will have the parents' wool colour. You can actually dye leather more colours than there are dyes, because you can mix different amounts of different dyes with the leather piece. You can wash leather of its dye with a water-filled cauldron.

You can dye leather thousands of different colours by using more than one dye in the crafting screen.

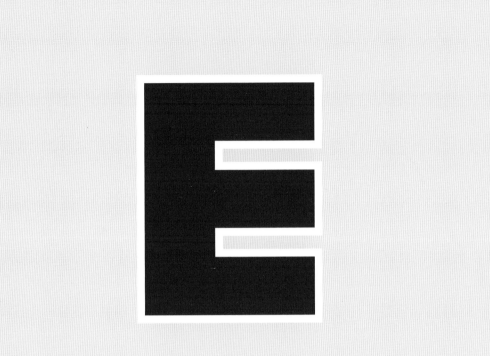

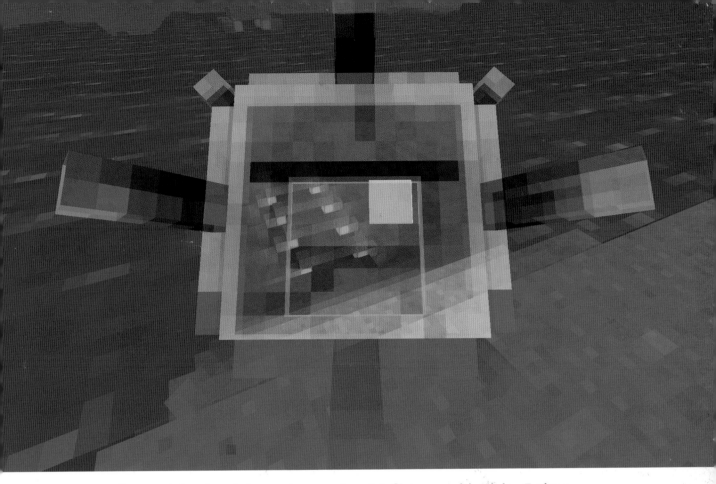

The elder guardian sends its ghostly image to you when it inflicts you with Mining Fatigue.

ELDER GUARDIAN

The elder guardian is a larger and more deadly version of the guardian, the underwater hostile mob that guards ocean monuments. Three elder guardians spawn with each ocean monument, and they will not respawn if you kill them. You will find them inside the monument, one in a central room near the monument's treasure and the other two in opposite sides of the structure.

The elder guardian behaves pretty much the same way as the guardian. However, it is much stronger and deals more damage. It can also in-flict players within fifty blocks with Mining Fatigue III for five minutes (it appears like a ghost on your screen when it does this). This makes it difficult to break blocks. The elder gives the same drops as a guardian but can also drop a wet sponge. You can dry a wet sponge in a fur-nace to create a dry sponge that will soak up many blocks of water. A dry sponge is useful for clearing out a pond or an ocean monument.

To fight a guardian, you will need enchanted armour and/or potions for fighting and moving underwater: Aqua Affinity, Respiration, and Depth Strider enchantments, and potions of

Swiftness, Night Vision, and Water Breathing. Because guardians and elder guardians move away so quickly, it's best to try to rush them into a corner where they can't escape, then strike them with your strongest sword.

ELYTRA

If you've ever wondered what it would be like to fly, place a pair of Elytra in the chestplate slot, jump in midair and let your character soar. Of course, to get the Elytra, you'll have to find an end ship in the End city and defeat the shulker guard first. One pair of Elytra will give you seven minutes and eleven seconds flying time, but they can be enchanted with Unbreaking or Mending to get more time in the air.

EMERGENCY SHELTERS

If you're caught outside, far from home at night, you may find you need to build a shelter from mobs, fast. One option is to dig into a mountain and close up the entrance for a quick shelter. You can also almost always dig three blocks down and place dirt blocks above you. You can also pillar jump with dirt or gravel blocks fifteen blocks up (to stay out of the range of skeleton arrows). If

The only way to gather cobwebs to use them later is with shears or a sword enchanted with Silk Touch in Creative mode or using commands.

you have a boat, you can boat away from shore. You can also place blocks around you and above you just to prevent mobs from damaging you.

ENCHANTING

Enchanting your weapons and armour gives you extra power and protection against your enemies, and enchanting your mining tools can help you mine, dig, and chop to get more loot faster. To enchant an item, you use an enchantment table or an anvil.

It costs experience points (XP) to enchant (and lapis with the enchantment table), and you'll need thirty experience levels for the top level enchantments. The higher experience level you are at, the more points you need to reach each new level. Because of this, the most efficient way to get the best enchantments from an enchantment table is to level up your XP to thirty, enchant one item, and then level back up to thirty. If you are not getting the enchantments you want, it can be worthwhile to enchant something cheap, like a stone sword, with a Level I enchantment. Doing this will reset the enchantments being offered. You can also trade with a villager to get enchanted tools and weapons.

You can also enchant books. This can be a great way to save enchantments to apply later with the anvil and it allows you to have a selection of enchantments you can choose from.

Different materials are more enchantable than others. Gold has the most enchantability, followed by diamond, chain, iron, stone, leather, and lastly wood. So if you really need a Respiration helmet fast, and you don't care how long it lasts, you might want to try a gold helmet on your enchantment table.

ENCHANTMENTS

You can enchant tools, weapons, and armour in Minecraft to make them stronger or give them special abilities. An enchantment can have different levels, up to Level V, although some enchantments only have one level and many only up to a Level III.

GENERAL ARMOUR ENCHANTMENTS are Blast (explosion) Protection, Fire Protection, Projectile Protection, Protection, and Thorns. Of the four protection enchantments, only Protection helps you with all types of damage. With an enchanted table you can only place Thorns on chestplates, but with an enchanted book and anvil you can place Thorns on other armour as well. Thorns will damage a mob or player when they attack you, but they also reduce your armour's durability.

HELMET ENCHANTMENTS are Aqua Affinity (which helps with mining speeds underwater) and Respiration (which helps you breathe longer and see more clearly underwater).

BOOT ENCHANTMENTS are Depth Strider (which allows you to move faster underwater), Feather Falling (which reduces fall damage), and Frost Walker (which turns water into a walkable ice surface).

SWORD ENCHANTMENTS are Sharpness (which increases damage the sword can inflict), Smite (which increases damage to the undead, like zombies, skeletons, and Withers),

Bane of Arthropods (which increases damage to spiders, silverfish, and endermites), Knockback (which knocks enemies back further), Fire Aspect (which lights any mobs but Nether mobs on fire), and Looting (which increases your target's loot drop if they die). While Knockback might seem advantageous, at higher (stronger) levels it can make it more difficult to kill a mob, because they are knocked back so far that you then have to move to get closer and continue fighting. Likewise with Fire Aspect – a mob aflame rushing to you can catch you on fire too!

You can also enchant an axe on an anvil with Bane of Arthropods, Sharpness, and Smite.

BOW ENCHANTMENTS are Power (which allows the bow to inflict more damage), Punch (which allows you to punch with more knockback), Flame (which sets your target on fire, except for Nether mobs), and Infinity (which allows you to access infinite arrows as long as you have at least one in your inventory).

TOOL ENCHANTMENTS (axe, pickaxe, and shovel) include Efficiency (mining faster), Silk Touch (which allows whole blocks to be dropped rather than just their item drops), and Fortune (which increases block drops). Fortune on a tool will get you more coal, diamond, emerald, Nether quartz, and lapis, but not more iron or gold, as these don't drop anything other than the block. The Fortune enchantment also works for getting more apples, carrots, flint, glowstone, melons, Nether wart, potatoes, saplings, sea lanterns, and wheat seeds. You can also place Efficiency and Silk Touch on shears using a book and the anvil.

FISHING ROD ENCHANTMENTS are Lure (more fish will bite, and there will be a slight decrease in catching junk or treasure) and Luck of the Sea (which creates a greater chance of catching treasure and less chance of catching junk).

THE GENERAL ENCHANTMENT UNBREAKING (which increases the lifespan of an object) can be placed on any tool, weapon, or armour. For shears, hoes, flint and steel, and carrot on a stick, you'll have to use an enchanted book.

THE MENDING ENCHANTMENT is a treasure enchantment that lets you "buy" repairs using experience (XP) points. When you hold an enchanted item, XP orbs that you've collected will repair it for you.

Some enchantments conflict with each other and can't be placed on the same item. You can only have one type of protection enchantment on a piece of armour, and you can't have Silk Touch and Fortune on the same tool. For your sword, you can't have more than one of Bane of Arthropods, Sharpness, or Smite.

ENCHANTMENT TABLE

Right-click the enchantment table to open the enchantment screen. This has a slot to place an item, a slot for adding lapis, and three buttons that show your enchantment choices. Tooltips will show you one enchantment that you'd get with each button, but you may get more. Each choice shows the number of experience levels

To get the highest level enchantments from an enchanting table, surround it with fifteen bookshelves, one block away. You can have more than fifteen, for looks, and chests to hold enchanted gear and books are always helpful.

that enchantment costs. If your bar shows you are at Level 30, and the third enchantment costs three, then you will drop to experience Level 27 once you click the bottom button to enchant the item. The enchantment choices shown are fairly random, except that they can't conflict with any existing enchantment on the item.

To get the highest level enchantments from a table, you will have to place bookshelves (up to fifteen) around the table. There must be one block of space between each bookshelf and the enchantment table, and they must be at the same height or one block above the table. You can disable a bookshelf's effects by placing a torch on the side of the bookshelf facing the table.

THE END

The End is another dimension in Minecraft, like the Nether. It is an island made of a special block called End stone and it is surrounded by many smaller, distant outer islands which you can get to through end gateway portals. If you fall off the edges of the island and into the Void, you will die. Tall columns of obsidian rise from the ground in the End. The End is the home of the Ender Dragon, the main boss of Minecraft, as well as Endermen. To get to the End, you must find and repair an End portal. When you use the portal, you will often arrive at a separate platform from the

The End is an island floating in the Void and populated by Endermen.

main End island. You need to bring along blocks (preferably obsidian) to bridge to the main island. There are only two ways back from the End: either kill the Dragon and return via a portal, or die. When you go through the exit portal back to the Overworld, you'll see a screen with a long poem about Minecraft. It's well worth reading!

END BIOME

The natural landscape of the End is programmed as a biome too, just like the Desert and Savanna Biomes. It's classed in the game as a cold biome, like a taiga biome, though it doesn't rain or snow in the End. It is the only place an Ender Dragon or Ender crystals can spawn, and the only biome that End stone appears in. There is no day or night in the End, which is a good thing because beds in the End explode when you try to use them.

END CITY

An end gateway portal sends you to an outer island that may contain an End city. The End city is made up of End stone bricks, chorus trees and purpur blocks and is lit by End rods. Finding one of the rare End cities is an adventure in itself. Explore the rooms to discover treasure chests and ender chests. But beware, innocent looking purpur blocks in the walls of the city may really be the shell of a hostile shulker!

END CRYSTAL

An Ender Dragon can recharge its health as it passes within 32 blocks of an End crystal. End crystals will explode if attacked. Placing four End crystals on each corner of the exit portal respawns the Ender Dragon.

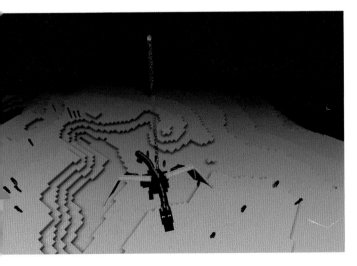

Crystal blocks send healing rays to the Ender Dragon as it passes by.

ENDER DRAGON

The Ender Dragon is the largest mob in the game, over twenty blocks long. It flies between special obsidian columns that have healing blocks of crystals on top of them. These crystals regenerate the dragon's health (a whopping one hundred hearts) when it is injured, making it very difficult to kill. You can see when an Ender Dragon is close by its purple health bar that appears on your screen. It will fly right at you and destroy any blocks in its way, except for obsidian and End stone. To defeat the Dragon, you first want to destroy its healing crystals, preferably with a bow and arrow or snowballs and eggs, as they explode powerfully when they break. Then fire arrows at the Dragon, trying to hit its head, as this causes it the most damage. Unless there are several of you fighting the Dragon, it will take quite a while to kill. The Ender Dragon is immune to lava, potions, and fire. You can only damage the Ender Dragon with explosions or arrows. During the fight, it can be tricky to avoid aggravating Endermen—wearing a pumpkin as a helmet will allow you to look at them without retaliation. But the pumpkin also makes it difficult to see. One option is to bring the makings of snow and iron golems to distract and kill as many Endermen as possible. An Ender Dragon death is a great spectacle of flashing rays and masses of experience orbs. It leaves behind an exit portal and a single Dragon Egg. So far, there

Endermen pick up more than dirt; they'll carry off cactus, flowers, melons, and TNT, too.

is no use for this egg except as a trophy. If you click the egg, it will teleport several blocks away, so it is difficult to collect. Use a piston to make it drop so you can pick it up. Make sure to cover the portal when you do this so it doesn't drop in there. Respawning the dragon will give you 500 XP and will reset the pillars and End crystals.

ENDERMEN

Endermen are three-block-tall mobs with very long arms and legs that leave purple sparkly trails. They randomly pick up certain blocks, like cac-

tus, clay, dirt varieties, flowers, mushrooms, gravel, melons, sand, and TNT, and randomly place them back down. They are neutral unless you look at them (put your crosshair) between their upper legs and head. They teleport away from damage, and water and rain damage them. If you attack them, they will teleport away, often behind you. However, they don't teleport if you are only looking at their legs. Because they are three blocks tall, a good way to fight them is to get under a two-block-high ledge and look at them to anger them. Then strike their feet with your sword. They'll sometimes drop Ender pearls when they die.

ENDER PEARLS

Ender pearls are dropped by Endermen when they are killed. You use them to create Eyes of Ender to find the End portal, but you can also use them to teleport. Just throw them at the block you want to teleport to. You will take five points damage when you teleport. When you throw them, there is a one in twenty chance the pearl may also spawn endermites, a tiny hostile, purple, silverfish-like creature.

END GATEWAY PORTAL

Each time the Ender Dragon is defeated, a new End gateway portal is generated that takes you to the outer islands and End cities. Throwing an Ender pearl into the portal will teleport you to the outer End islands.

END PORTAL

The End portal that takes you to the End is found in

The End portal room in a stronghold has a portal placed over lava and a silverfish spawner.

You get most XP for killing hostile mobs, but you can still do well breeding and killing passive mobs. To breed large numbers of mobs, stand on a block so it's easier to see.

an underground stronghold. There are three strongholds generated with each world. To find them, you can use Eyes of Ender (Ender pearls crafted with blaze powder) by throwing them in the air. The Eyes travel in the direction you must go, and when you are over the stronghold, they drop down into the ground. Dig down to find the stronghold, then explore to find the End portal room. The End portal is missing several Eyes of Ender needed to make it work. You'll need sixteen or so Eyes of Ender to find the stronghold and then repair it when you get there. There is also a silverfish spawner in the portal room that you will need to break or disable.

END SHIP

You can teleport to this rare floating pirate ship located near to End cities using an ender pearl. Once aboard, you'll find a brewing stand with healing potions, two treasure chests, a dragon head, and a pair of Elytra. To access the treasure and wings, you'll need to defeat the shulker guard first.

EXPERIENCE

When you do certain activities in Minecraft, you receive experience points, or XP, that can show

You'll find mountains of gravel and more trees in the Extreme Hills+ M Biome.

up as floating green orbs. You get XP from killing mobs (but not baby animals, bats, golems, or villagers), mining (but not iron or gold), using the furnace, fishing, trading, and breeding animals. These points fill up your experience bar, and when the bar is filled, you gain a new level. Above Level 15, you need ever-increasing XP to reach the next level. Experience points are only used for enchanting and the anvil.

You'll get the most experience points from killing hostile mobs (especially if they are wearing armour), destroying mob spawners, and from breaking a bottle o' enchanting (trade with villagers for this). Mining Nether quartz also gives a fair amount of XP. You can build a mob XP farm to gather many hostile mobs in an enclosed area that has barricades to protect you while you kill them for the XP. You can also set up a farm to breed and kill lots of animals for XP.

EXTREME HILLS BIOME

The Extreme Hills Biome is a great location to go mining and caving. First off, there are more cave systems in an Extreme Hills Biome. It is also the only biome where you can mine emeralds or be bothered by silverfish. Because of the cliffs and exposed rock in the Extreme Hills Biome, you can also easily find ore exposed overground. This can be very handy if you are just starting out and in need of coal quickly. Variations of Extreme Hills Biomes are Extreme Hills M Biome, which has higher mountains and mountains made of gravel, and Extreme Hills+ Biome, which has more spruce and oak trees. Extreme Hills+ M Biome has the enormous gravel mountains as well as more trees and grass.

To help crops grow faster, plant them next to other crops, in rows, and keep them lit at night.

FARMING

It can take two to three Minecraft days for a crop of potatoes, beetroot, carrots, or wheat to fully grow. To make your crops grow as fast as they can, make sure the farmland is watered and that your crops have light during the night. To water the farmland, there must be a source of water within four blocks. A standard tactic is to make a 9x9 block of farmland, with the centre block dug out and filled with water. Crops also grow faster if they are planted next to other types of crops, so having rows of different crops will help. Keeping the blocks at the edge of your farm plots empty and watered will also help crops grow faster. Also, when you are about one hundred blocks from your farm, growth stops. So if you are in a rush for carrots, stay close by.

Alternating Nether fence posts with regular fence posts will let you walk through, but not sheep, pigs, or cows.

FENCES

Fences are programmed as one and a half blocks high, so most mobs can't get over them. This includes you, unless you have potions or status effects. Wood fences don't connect to Nether brick fences, so, if you alternate the two, you can walk through, but sheep, pigs, and cows can't. You can also put a block of carpet on a fence to get over it quickly.

FIGHTING

Fighting tactics, whether you are fighting mobs or PvP (Player versus Player—other players in the game), include blocking, block-hitting, critical hits, encircling, knockback, and strafing. You can prevent up to 50 per cent of damage from an incoming strike by using a shield. However, blocking with a shield causes you to move slowly, so this isn't a good tactic if you need to run.

You can knock your target back further if you sprint and then hit it, or by hitting it with snowballs or eggs. Knocking back skeletons however, gives them more opportunity to recharge their bows and fire at you, so this isn't a good tactic to use with skeletons. Circling around your target to attack its back gives a skeleton less opportunity to hit you. Strafing (moving left and right with your A and D keys) also makes you difficult to hit. Also don't forget to use critical hits when you can, by jumping and then striking as you drop. Another important aspect to battle is food. You heal much more quickly when your hunger bar is full, so keep good food (steaks, chops) on your hotbar for a long battle.

FIREWORKS

Fireworks don't serve any purpose other than fun, and they don't do any damage when they explode. But they make a nice bang and look awesome. To create fireworks, first make

To make basic fireworks, all you need is gunpowder, paper, and dye.

a coloured firework star with one gunpowder and one dye. You can modify the firework by adding a diamond to create trails or glowstone dust for a twinkle. You can also choose a shape: add a fire charge for a bigger sphere, a gold nugget for a star shape, a feather for a burst, or any mob head for a creeper head shape. To make the final rocket, combine your custom firework star with one paper and one gunpowder. Add one or two more gunpowder for more height, and additional stars for more explosions! Set these off outside by right-clicking to place them.

FISHING

Fishing is a really good way to get food quickly, and you can fish in just a single block of water or a waterfall. You can even fish inside and underground, although fish will bite less often. Fish will take the bait most often when it's raining. Your chances actually improve during

Set your enemies on fire by clicking a flint and steel at their feet.

FLINT AND STEEL

rain by about 20 per cent. You can catch more than fish, too. You have a 10 per cent chance of catching junk (bowls, leather, squid ink sacs, leather boots, sticks, string, damaged bows and fishing rods, tripwire hooks, water bottles, and bones) and a 5 per cent chance of catching treasure (saddles, lily pads, name tags, enchanted-but-used bows and fishing rods, and enchanted books). This can really help you out in early game.

Flint and steel is a tool you make from an iron ingot and flint. You click it on a block to set the block on fire. Click the ground under mobs or players, or the blocks in front of them if they're running, to set them on fire. Setting a cow, pig, sheep, or rabbit on fire to kill it will cause the animal to drop cooked meat.

Flower Forest Biomes are a relatively rare variant of the Forest Biome.

FLOWER FOREST BIOME

In a Flower Forest Biome, you'll find every type of flower except for the blue orchid, the chorus flower, and the sunflower. The blue orchid can be found in the swamplands, the chorus flower is found in the End, and the sunflower is found in sunflower plains. The Flower Forest Biome is the best place to start a flower farm!

FLOWERS

As previously mentioned, different flowers generate in different biomes in Minecraft. Using bone meal on grass will not only generate tall grass but also one or more of that biome's flowers. You can't use bone meal to generate any of the large flowers: sunflowers, rose bushes, peonies, and lilacs. However, you can use bone meal on any of these tall flowers and they will drop a clone!

To get more of the four tall flowers in Minecraft (peonies, sunflowers, lilacs, and rose bushes), you'll need to right-click one with bone meal.

Sunflowers can also help you navigate—they always face east.

FOREST BIOME

The Forest Biome is very common, and a good place to start out in, as it gives you access to lots of wood. In addition to plentiful oak trees and some birch trees, you can find poppies, dandelions, mushrooms, and tall grass here.

As with any forest, the canopy of leaves can make the area dark enough for mobs to spawn easily, so torch up your home to keep it safe. The Forest Biome is also smaller than many others, so you may not have to travel far to get to another biome.

A variant of the Forest Biome is the Forest Hills Biome, which is identical except that it has a more rugged terrain.

FUEL

You are not limited to using coal in a furnace. You can also use buckets of lava, blaze rods, charcoal, saplings, and mushroom blocks. Lava, blaze rods, and blocks of coal are more efficient than coal, but you need to keep an eye out to make sure you keep putting smeltable items in the furnace while lava and blaze rods are burning. You can also use many items that are made of wood, including banners, bookshelves, chests, crafting tables, fences, planks, sticks, and wood tools and weapons.

GAME MODE

Minecraft has different modes you choose at the start. They are designed for the different types of gameplay. In Survival, you have to find food and survive mob attacks. You can be killed, but you have multiple or infinite lives. You respawn at your starting point (losing your experience points and inventory possessions). Hardcore is the same as Survival, except you play at the hardest difficulty and

See the world like a creeper does by clicking on one in Spectator mode.

A ghost's fireballs can be deadly, but they are also slow, and you can also volley them back at the ghast.

you only have one life. When you die, your world is deleted.

Adventure mode is designed for playing adventure maps made by others. You can't break or destroy many blocks, but you can still fight mobs, explore, and do things like eat and open doors.

In Spectator mode, you can fly around and through blocks, but you can't interact with any blocks. You can, however, click a mob and see the world through its eyes. Try a spider, creeper, or Enderman!

In Creative mode, you can fly (but not through blocks) and you have a special item selection screen that gives you access to almost all of the blocks in Minecraft. Mobs can't harm you. Creative mode is a great mode if you just want to concentrate on building.

You set your game mode when you start a world, and if you want to change it during play, you need to start your world with cheats enabled. To change game mode midstream, open chat (press T) and type /gamemode followed by a space and the code for the mode you want: for Survival: **survival**, or the shortcuts **s** or **0**; for Creative: **creative**, **c**, or **1**; for Adventure: **adventure**, **a**, or **2**; and for Spectator: **spectator**, **sp**, or **3**.

GHASTS

Ghasts are one of the largest mobs, and one of the deadliest. They can track you from a hundred blocks away, although they don't start firing until you are within about sixty blocks. Their explosive fireballs can give you as much as fifteen and a half hearts damage if you are in Hard difficulty. However their fireballs move pretty slowly, so you can usually step out of the way. With a little practice, it's fairly easy to send a fireball back at a ghast with any tool, and you can even use your fist, a snowball, or an arrow. If you do hit a ghast with its own fireball, you'll get the achievement Return to Sender. To stop a ghast firing at you, just step out of its sight; they'll only fire if they can see you. If you are playing in the Nether a lot, make tunnels and walls of cobble to prevent ghasts from seeing you.

If you want to make Regeneration potions, you'll need the rare drop of ghast tears to make them. Ghasts only have ten health points (five hearts), so one strike from an enchanted bow can kill them.

GOLDEN APPLES

Golden apples are a great way to get potion-like healing before you have access to potion-making ingredients. There are two types of golden apples – the golden apple and the enchanted golden apple. A golden apple is crafted with an apple and eight gold ingots. Enchanted golden apples can be found in dungeon, desert temple, and mineshaft chests.

Both types of golden apples give you four hunger points and about nine saturation points, as well as two minutes of Absorption. Absorption from a golden apple gives you two additional hearts on your health bar, coloured gold. The regular golden apple also gives five seconds of Regeneration. The enchanted golden apple (sometimes called a Notch apple) gives you a stronger Regeneration effect for twenty seconds and Absorption for two minutes, as well as Fire Resistance and Resistance (reduced damage) for five minutes. Overall, you can gain as many as two hundred health points regenerated by eating an enchanted

You can't dodge a guardian's rays, but you can stop them from firing by moving out of sight.

golden apple. You use a regular golden apple to heal a zombie villager, and you can use either type to help tame and breed horses, and to mature foals.

GUARDIANS

Guardians are underwater fish-like mobs that spawn around an ocean monument. They have retractable spikes and use a laser beam to attack both players and squid. While a guardian charges its laser, the beam is purple; when it's fully charged and able to damage you, the laser turns yellow. The guardian does need to be within about fifteen blocks of you and in line of sight to zap you with up to nine points of damage (on Hard difficulty). And when you attack back, it can give you two more points of damage through its spikes, if they are extended.

Because arrows don't fly well underwater, you'll want to attack the guardian with a sharp sword. Also, since guardians can dart away so quickly, try to corner them so they can't move while you hit them. And of course, to fight underwater you'll need potions and armour enchantments. Elder guardians are a larger, stronger, and rarer mini-boss variant of the guardian.

Your HUD shows your health bar, hunger bar, experience bar, your status effect, and your inventory hotbar.

HEADS-UP DISPLAY [HUD]

Your heads-up display, or HUD, is the display at the bottom of your screen that contains your health bar (in hearts), hunger bar (in shanks), your status effects (with positive effects on the top row and negative effects on the bottom), your experience bar, and your inventory hotbar. If you're underwater, your HUD will show how much air you have left, and if you are on a horse, it will show your horse's health instead of hunger. Status effects blink then fade out as they are depleted.

HEALTH

Each player and mob in Minecraft has a specific number of health points. Players have twenty health points, and these are represented in your heads-up display as hearts. Each heart is worth two points. The smallest slime block has one point (half of a heart) while the Wither has three hundred points (150 hearts). Once a player or mob has no health points left, they die. You do naturally regenerate health, but only when your hunger level is over eighteen points, or nine shanks. That's why it's important to keep eating during battles. You can also recover hearts or regenerate health points with potions (Healing and Regeneration), beacons (Regeneration), and golden apples (Regeneration and Absorption). If your health reaches as low as two points, your health bar will start shaking. You'll start losing health when your hunger is at zero.

HELL BIOME

The Hell Biome is the biome used by the Minecraft game programming to generate the Nether. It's classified as a dry/warm biome, like a Desert or Savanna. However, the Hell Biome differs from other biomes because it has a defined top and bottom. At Level 1 (the bottom) and Level 128 (the top) is bedrock. The bedrock ceiling is also covered by layers of netherrack. Lava oceans occur at Level 31, and there are plenty of fast-flowing lava springs and streams, and lakes, as well. The Hell

In older versions of Minecraft there were tricks you could use to break through bedrock. At the top of the Nether, you'd find a dark sky and some mushrooms. Mojang has fixed this as of version 1.8.3, although other tricks may yet be found.

Biome terrain is made mostly of highly flammable netherrack, with small clusters of Nether quartz, patches of soul sand, and layers of gravel, along with outcrops of exposed glowstone. The Hell Biome is also the only place that the Nether fortress, Nether brick, and Nether wart are found. It is also the only biome where Nether mobs (blazes, ghasts, wither skeletons, magma cubes, and zombie pigmen) spawn naturally. (Zombie pigmen can also spawn by a Nether portal in the Overworld.)

HIDDEN MOBS

There are three mobs in Minecraft that never ap-

Giant zombies look nice, but they just stand around.

pear in the regular game, but you can summon them with cheats or commands. You can summon a giant zombie, twelve blocks high, with the command /summon Giant. (It doesn't do anything but look giant though.) You can also summon a skeleton horse with /summon EntityHorse ~ ~ ~ {Type:4} and a zombie horse with /summon EntityHorse ~ ~ ~ {Type:3}. Both horses have twenty-six hearts of health, but neither can be tamed, although you can summon tamed versions by adding a comma and Tame:1 after the Type declaration in the command /summon EntityHorse~ ~ ~ {Type:4, Tame:1}. Both horses behave similarly to regular horses, but the zombie horse drops rotten flesh and the skeleton

Zombie and skeleton horses are in the game's programming, but not in the game.

drops bones. Also, you can't use a lead on them, nor can you feed or breed them.

All horse armour—iron, gold, and diamond—is impossible to damage.

HORSE ARMOUR

You can't craft horse armour, but you can find it in chests or trade with villagers for it. More specifically, you can find horse armour in chests that are found in dungeons and temples or in village blacksmith shops. There are three types of horse armour: iron armour gives the horse 20 per cent protection, gold gives 28 per cent, and diamond gives 44 per cent. Although you can't enchant it, horse armour has unlimited durabil-ity, so you never have to repair it.

HORSES

Riding a horse may be the fastest way to travel in Survival mode. Some horses can jump over five blocks high and across ten-block gaps. Different horses have different jumping abilities, speed, and health. They may jump anywhere from a little over a block to five and a half blocks. Their health can be between fifteen and thirty hearts. Their speed

Horses can be one of seven colours—white, buckskin, bay, dark bay, black, chestnut, and grey—and can also have a type of marking: blaze and stockings, paint, snowflake appaloosa, and sooty.

can be from around a player's walking speed to up to three times faster. A foal will have a combination of their parents' characteristics, but this is mixed with some randomization so that it is tricky to breed horses for improved traits.

Horses don't like water, so they'll throw you off if you enter water that is three blocks deep. You'll need a lead to get them through deep water. Because they are vulnerable to wandering into water and lava pools, leash your horses to a fencepost with a lead or put them in a safe enclosure.

You can fight on horses, just like on foot, and you can also mine and collect dropped items while on a horse. You breed horses with golden apples or carrots. You can also feed damaged horses to heal them with wheat, sugar, apples, bread, and hay bales. (If the horse isn't damaged, you'll just end up mounting it.) These foods will also cause a foal to mature faster.

On occasion, a horse will be struck by lightning and turned into a skeleton trap horse and rider. Three more horsemen will appear nearby, equipped with enchanted helmets and arrows. Once you defeat them, you can ride their horses which have already been tamed. When you ride a horse, your hunger bar is replaced with its health bar, and its jump bar is above your experience bar. To jump a horse, press the space bar until the jump bar fills up, and then release.

HUNGER

If you are playing in Survival mode on any difficulty beyond Peaceful, you will need to make sure you never get too hungry. Being too hungry drops your health points, and you have to have at least nine shanks to regenerate health. In Hard difficulty you can even die from starvation—you start taking damage when your hunger bar gets to zero. More strenuous activities will increase your hunger faster: sprinting, jumping, fighting, being damaged, swimming, and breaking blocks. If your hunger bar is six points or less, you won't be able to sprint at all.

The food items you prepare or gather in Minecraft all have different values for combating hunger, and in general cooked food satisfies your hunger more than raw. In addition to the hunger bar, you also have a hidden score for saturation. It's only when your saturation reaches zero that your hunger bar starts going down. Each type of food has a different number for its hunger points and its saturation points. The more saturation points a food has, the longer it will keep your hunger bar full (you won't get hungry as quickly). The top foods for restoring both hunger and saturation points are: rabbit stew, steak, pork chops, and golden carrots.

In an emergency, to prevent starvation, you can eat raw chicken, rotten meat, poisonous potatoes, and even spider eyes. They will give you poisoning too, but you will recover if you are healthy.

ICE PLAINS SPIKES BIOME

The Ice Plains Spikes Biome is a rare version of the Ice Plains Biome. You won't find much to help you survive, but you will find magnificent spikes of packed ice. Packed ice, unlike regular ice, is not transparent and won't melt when light sources are nearby. It also doesn't drop water like regular ice when broken. But like regular ice, packed ice is slippery, so you sprint faster and slide on it, and is great for making speedy tunnels to sprint through. You have to mine it with a Silk Touch pickaxe.

The fantastic landscape in an Ice Plains Spikes Biome offers all the packed ice you could want.

IGLOOS

Igloos spawn in Ice Plains and Cold Taiga. Each one holds a large amount of loot, including carpets, a redstone torch, bed, furnace, and crafting table. Some also have a mossy brick basement complete with brewing material, zombies and silverfish. Use the golden apple you find in the chest and the Weakness potion to turn one of the zombies back into a villager.

INVENTORY

Your inventory can get pretty crowded as you play, and there are several shortcuts you can use to work with your inventory faster, so that you don't have to drag and drop everything. Press 1 to 9 to access the items in your hotbar. Press Shift and click on an item to move a stack of that item between your inventory and hotbar, or between a container and your hotbar or inventory. Move items between the inventory and a specific slot in your hotbar by hovering over the item or blank slot in the inventory and

There are many shortcuts you can use to move items or stacks of items between your hotbar (the row of your inventory that appears on the HUD for easy access) and your inventory.

pressing the number for that slot, from 1 to 9. Right-click an item to pick up half a stack. Double-click an item in your inventory to pick up as many as available (up to a full stack). To move as many items or stacks of one kind as you can from your inventory to a chest, pick up any item, press Shift, and double-click the item you want to move. Right-click on an empty slot when you are holding a stack to drop just one item from it. Click and drag a stack of items to distribute the items equally between inventory slots. You can also right-click and drag over the slots to drop one item at a time into each slot. You can repeat this action multiple times. To craft as many items as possible from your crafting grid, shift-click in the crafted item slot.

IRON GOLEMS

Iron golems only spawn naturally if a village has at least ten villagers and twenty-one houses. They are a utility mob and protect villagers

d screenshot as 2015-02-22_15.59.14.png

iron golems will attack hostile mobs, except for creepers and wolves. Their punch is almost as powerful as a creeper's explosion.

by attacking any hostile mobs or neutral mobs within sixteen blocks. If you damage them or a villager, they will also attack you (unless you created them). If your local village doesn't have an iron golem, it's a good idea to make one or add enough houses and villagers to the village to help naturally spawn an iron golem.

You make an iron golem from four blocks of iron placed as a T on the ground, with a pumpkin or jack o' lantern on top for the head. Villagers don't need to be present for iron golems to attack mobs, so iron golems can also be handy as guards for your property. You can fence them in or leash them to stop them from wandering away. Iron golems aren't foolproof security for your villagers though, so a mob-proof wall and lighting are still essential protections.

J, K, L

JUNGLE BIOME

The Jungle Biome isn't a very common biome – you'll often have to search a bit for it. This is the only biome in which you can find jungle temples, jungle trees, ocelots, cocoa pods, and melons. You'll also find ferns, flowers, and vines here. Most of the ground is covered by jungle bushes, which are really one-block-high jungle wood covered by oak leaves. Variations of the Jungle Biome include the more mountainous Jungle M Biome, the hillier Jungle Hills Biome, and the Jungle Edge Biome. The Jungle Edge Biome is only occasionally generated, between regular Jungle or Jungle M Biomes and other biomes, and is not as dense as a Jungle Biome. It is very rare that you'll find the Jungle Edge M Biome, a mix of the Jungle Edge Biome and the Jungle M Biome.

A Jungle Edge M Biome like this is rare to find, as it's a variant of the less dense Jungle Edge Biome that only sometimes appears at the border of a jungle.

Jungle temples are often well hidden in the trees and often partially buried.

JUNGLE TEMPLES

You can find rare loot in jungle temples, as well as some booby traps. In a jungle temple there are two chests with random goods as with the desert temple. One chest is hidden between floors and the other is protected by two automatic arrow dispensers. To open the hidden chest, you have to solve a lever puzzle on the bottom floor. The solution depends on what side of the temple the puzzle is on. Click the outermost lever, then the innermost, and then the middle. Then click the middle, the innermost, and then the outermost. Go up the stairs and see a space opened up above the chest. To get to the other chest, you have to disable two tripwire traps to stop the automatic arrow dispensers. One is in the corridor approaching the room the chest is in, and another in the room with the chest. To disable a tripwire, break the string placed on the floor between two tripwire hooks.

The Killer Bunny

The killer bunny attacks players and wolves.

KILLER BUNNY

The killer bunny is a very rare hostile rabbit, with one in a thousand chance of spawning. It is white with horizontal red eyes. Its name, the killer bunny, is also displayed above it! Don't mix it up with the white rabbits with vertical red eyes which aren't hostile. The killer bunny will attack players and wolves. It can give up to twelve points of damage on Hard difficulty, so

be quick about killing it before it kills you!

LADDERS

When you are climbing on a ladder, you can use the sneak key (the Shift key) to stop. You can mine or break blocks while you are stopped, but not as fast. You can stand on top of the narrow top side of a ladder, and you can jump to this top area from other blocks. Placing a ladder block (or

You can jump onto the top edge of a ladder – know how to do this for parkour maps!

a fence block) underwater will give you one block of breathing room. But ladders can't be placed on transparent blocks like glass or on leaves or slabs.

LAVA

Lava generates in Minecraft as lakes and rivers. Between Levels 1 and 10 (the lava level) are many pools of lava. You find lakes of different sizes at all levels, and if they are above ground they can cause forest fires. A lava source block can cause a nearby flammable block above it to catch fire if there is also an air block present. Single source blocks of lava will form rivers that fall down walls. If you can reach the source block, you can remove it with an empty bucket. Lava is a fluid like wa-

ter, but flows slower. It also only flows for three blocks in the Overworld. In the Nether, lava flows much faster and for seven blocks, like water. The only mobs not damaged by lava are Nether mobs, which are also immune to fire.

Lava has several very useful properties. If flowing water touches a stationary lava source, it creates obsidian from the lava source. (This feature allows you to create a portal without ever needing a diamond pickaxe.)

When lava flows on top of water, it creates stone. When lava touches flowing water, it creates cobblestone, without using up any lava or water. This means you can create a simple cobblestone generator very easily. In a four block long trench, place water

To make a cobble generator, dig a trench so that flowing lava meets water flowing down into a hole.

at one end and dig out an extra block in the second space for the water to flow down into. At the other end, place lava. That's it! When you dig out one cobble, another will form. To help make sure the cobble doesn't fall into the lava, you can place a hopper beneath the block where the cobble forms.

A bucket of lava can also be a great weapon in your inventory (though you have to be careful not to damage yourself when you pour it), and it can be used to fuel a furnace.

LIGHTING

Every block in Minecraft has a light level between zero and fifteen. Zero is dark, fifteen is the same as bright sunlight. Sunlight during rain or snow is twelve and during a thunderstorm is ten.

The light is very important in Minecraft because light decides when and where many hostile mobs spawn. When the light is above seven, in most cases no mobs will spawn. When the overall light is below seven (for example, at night time or in unlit caves), you can keep light above seven by placing torches every five or six blocks, staggering them in rows. A torch gives a brightness of fourteen, but each block you travel away from the light source, the light level drops by one, in each three dimensional direction. An End rod

Glowstone, redstone lamps, and jack o' lanterns give off more light than a torch.

has a light level of fourteen as well, and can also be used as a spiral staircase in some End city towers, can be moved by pistons, and will melt snow and ice within a two-block radius.

Some light sources like beacons, glowstone, redstone lamps, and jack o' lanterns have a brightness as high as fifteen. Furnaces give a light level of thirteen while they are smelting, and redstone torches and Ender chests give a level of seven. Mushrooms and brewing stands give a level of one. Glass allows full light to pass through, while water and ice will decrease the light by about two levels.

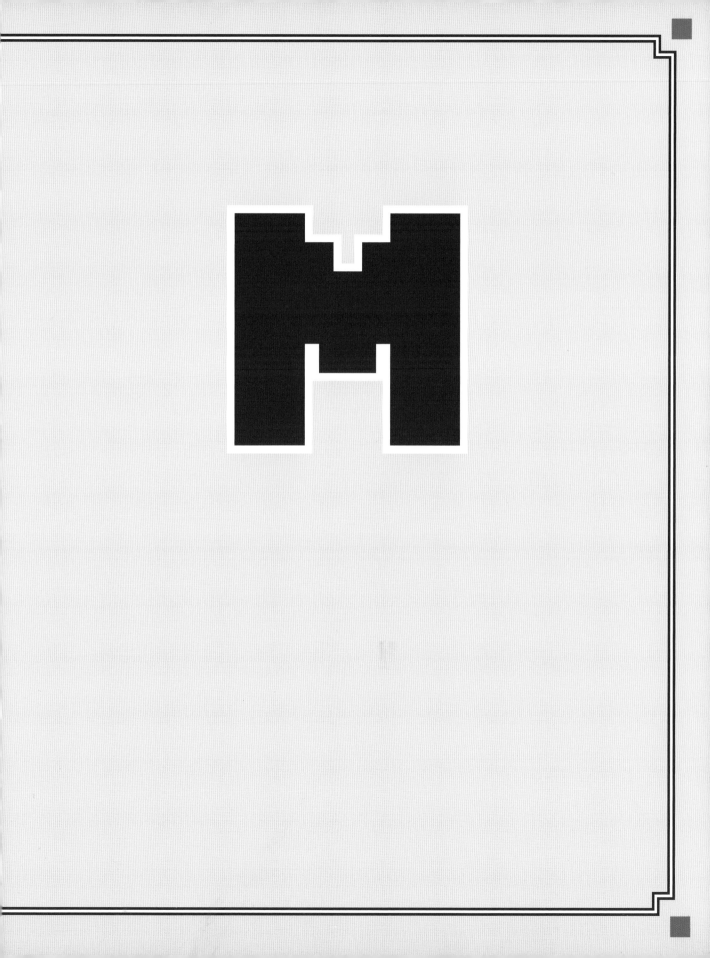

Magma cubes bounce like slimes and split into smaller cubes when you kill them.

MAGMA CUBES

Magma cubes are one of the rarer Nether mobs. They hop like slime, but are more dangerous. Magma cubes attack by trying to jump on top of you, and any contact is damaging. Use a bow to kill the big ones first, and then move back as it spawns littler ones when it dies. Wait to use your sword on the small ones. Magma cubes have hidden armour points, which make them harder to kill.

MAPS [IN-GAME MAPS]

When you first make a map it is empty. You have to right-click it for it to start mapping the area you are in. Lighter areas on a map are higher elevation areas. You can make maps at four different zoom levels. The standard map uses one pixel to show one block. To zoom out further, craft a map with eight pieces of paper around it. You can do this three times to

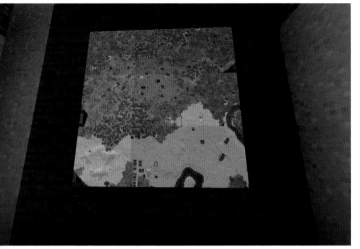

You can make a wall map with adjoining maps in item frames.

A version of Vech's Super Hostile Map, Spellbound, is available in Minecraft Realms. It features fantastic and terrifying locations where you must fight off hordes of mobs and find the treasure.

get to the most zoomed out level, which shows one pixel for every 16x16 blocks. The maps you make are designed so that they will align with the other maps you design. You make aligned additional maps when you enter a new area. You can duplicate a map by crafting it with a blank map.

When you place a map into an item frame, the frame disappears and the map takes up the whole side of the block. This lets you make seamless wall maps by placing adjacent maps next to each other in item frames. You can also make flat, horizontal pixel art on the ground and a map will display it. When one hand is occupied, a mini-map will be displayed. To view the large version, you need to hold the map in the main hand slot with both hands free.

MAPS [WORLD MAPS]

World maps are limited worlds created by other players or teams and often designed to give you special challenges. Some maps are designed for one or two players and you can download them to your PC. Public mini-game servers have special maps built for their games.

There are several different categories of maps that focus on different game elements. Adventure maps will have quests for you to do, and Survival maps will test your fighting and survival skills. Parkour maps test your ability to jump and move. Creative maps are built for you to explore and play in the custom scenery and buildings.

You can find many world maps at http://www.minecraftforum.net. Some maps use game mods (modification applications) or resource packs. You need to be sure you are running the same version of the game that the map uses, as well as any mods needed. It is very easy to install maps into your single-player game if they don't require extra mods. In your Minecraft application folder, you'll find a folder called Saves. Place unzipped map files in here.

Some of the most popular maps include: the Super Hostile map series by Vechs, SkyBlock by Noobcrew, the Diversity maps by qmagnet, Herobrine's Mansion by Hypixel, Hunger Games V2 multiplayer map by Wasted49, The Dropper by Bigre, Assassin's Creep by Selib, and Survival Island by Ashien. There are many more excellent maps by Minecraft players that you can find at the Minecraft Forum.

MEGA TAIGA BIOME

The Mega Taiga Biome is a rarer variation of the Taiga Biome, which has spruce trees and wolves. In the Mega Taiga Biome, you'll also find massive spruce trees, mossy boulders, podzol, and coarse dirt. Podzol is a type of dirt that doesn't grow grass but does let you grow mushrooms on it at any light level.

With its gigantic spruce trees, the Mega Taiga Biome has almost as much wood as a Jungle Biome.

MELONS AND PUMPKINS

You can find melon and pumpkin seeds in chests, buy them whole from villagers, or find melons and pumpkins growing naturally in the wild. You'll find melons only in jungles, while pumpkins can be found in many biomes. You will need to plant their seeds on farmland. You can't use bone meal to grow a full pumpkin or melon, but you can use it to grow the stem. To grow the most fruit from a melon or pumpkin, make sure that the stem is surrounded by watered farmland, with the four blocks at the sides of the stem empty.

MESA (BRYCE) BIOME

In a Mesa (Bryce) Biome, you'll find the same fea-

All Mesa Biomes have masses of clay, but the very rare Mesa (Bryce) features narrow, tall towers of clay.

tures as in a Mesa Biome – six colours of stained clay, hardened clay, red sand, red sandstone, cactus, and dead bushes. However, in the Mesa (Bryce) Biome you'll also find awesome spiky towers of clay.

MINECARTS

As well as the standard minecart you ride in, there is also the minecart with a furnace that can push carts in front of it, and a minecart with chest. A minecart with a hopper can gather items on the track or can be loaded with items from other containers. A minecart with TNT will explode when it runs over an activator rail, if it falls more than three blocks, or if it is hit by a flaming arrow. Minecarts don't attach to each other, but one can push the others in front.

Minecarts are a great way to move mobs to where you want them. In order to control the movement of the minecart, you'll have to place a rail down to set the minecart on, but then you can push the minecart where you want it. Push the minecart into the mob. Once the mob's in, you can set more rails to move them and the minecart wherever you want them. To get the mob out of the minecart, break the cart carefully so that you don't accidentally damage the mob, especially a villager if an iron golem is nearby.

MINI-GAMES

Mini-games are multiplayer games played on public Minecraft mini-game servers. There are many types of mini-games and many servers feature many of the different types. Popular types of mini-games include Hunger Games, Survival Games, Spleef, Hide and Seek, Cops n Robbers, the Walls, SkyWars, and Splegg. Free, public mini-game servers will often sell addi-

When you join a mini-game server, like The Hive at play.hivemc.com, you'll start in a lobby where you can choose what game you want to join.

tional vanity items, like pets, to make money, and they often have premium memberships that offer perks. Some mini-games are quite short, lasting ten minutes or less. When you log on to a mini-game server, you'll be in a lobby, or a series of lobbies, where you can choose what mini-games you want to play, then read the rules and pick a game to join.

MINING

All the different types of ore – from charcoal to diamond – are found between different levels in the ground. The bottom level in the Overworld is Level 0, the next block up is Level 1, then Level 2, and so forth. You can find diamond between Levels 1 and 15, emerald between 4 and 31, and coal on most levels. For the greatest chance of finding all the rarer ores, as well as common ores, dig at Level 11. To see what level you are at, open up your debug screen by pressing F3 and look at your x-, y-, and z-coordinates: the y-coordinate shows what level your feet are in. You can also just dig down to bedrock and then count up the blocks from there. If you are really intent on finding all diamonds, make three levels of branch mines on Levels 6, 10, and 14. However, at Level 10 and below

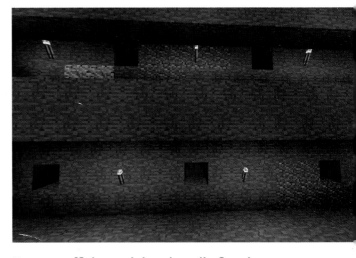

For very efficient mining, just dig five deep one-block holes every five or six blocks along a main walkway. Place your walkways twelve or thirteen blocks from each other, and leave a couple of blocks between levels.

you'll start finding a lot of lava pools, so bring a bucket of water. Branch mines are small 2x1 mining tunnels that branch out from a main passageway. To extract every ore from an area, you can place branch mines every third block, so that there are only two blocks between them. However, you can also put three blocks between the mines, and you'll rarely miss anything.

If you can accept a little bit of loss, the most efficient way to find the most ore in the least amount of time (outside of caving, which is the most effective way to mine) is to increase the number of blocks between mined strips to about five or six. Some statistical modelling shows that this yields the most ore per minute. Taking this to an extreme, dig 1x1 horizontal shafts five blocks deep every five or six blocks from a main mining corridor. Do this on levels above and below, leaving three or four blocks between levels and staggering the holes. On the same level, make your main mining corridors that you walk along fifteen blocks or so apart. Regardless of your method, when you find ore, dig the blocks out all around it, because some ore blocks are diagonal to each other, rather than side by side.

MOBS

The word *mob* is short for mobile. Mobile was used in early multiplayer gaming to describe any entity that could move. In Minecraft, mobs are categorized as passive (they'll never attack, like chickens and sheep), hostile (always attack), and neutral (attack only under certain conditions). The neutral mobs are Endermen, wolves, spiders (because they only turn hostile at a light level of seven or below), and zombie pigmen. Some mobs are also classed as tameable (ocelots, wolves, donkeys, mules, skeleton horses, and horses). Two others, iron golems and snow golems, are called utility mobs. You can create them, and they carry out a useful purpose. There are also two boss mobs in Minecraft, the Ender Dragon and the Wither. They're called boss mobs because they are so much more powerful than regular mobs and they also have a more complicated behaviour.

Hostile mobs spawn in areas that are at least twenty-four blocks away from players, but within 128 blocks. Once they spawn, they walk around randomly for several seconds. If they see a player within sixteen blocks of them (some can see further), they will start to pursue. If there's no one within thirty-two blocks, they'll just stand around. If there aren't any players within 128 blocks, they will despawn (disappear).

MODPACKS

Modpacks are groups of mods (modifications) hand-selected to play together. Some modpacks include quests programmed by their creator. Some may emphasize a certain type of mod, like technical mods you use to help mine and manage ores, or magical mods that let you gather resources and powers through altars, spells, and the like. Modpacks are the easiest way to get started playing with mods, because they've been preselected not to conflict with each other. The Feed the Beast (FTB) Launcher and the Technic Launcher are modpack launchers that help you install and

The popular modpack Attack of the B-Team, created by Technic, was designed to let you play as a crazy, mad scientist with the emphasis on crazy and mad. It has mods that add unusual new creatures, extraordinary hats, dragons you can ride, minions, and the ability to morph into any creature you have killed.

NOTE Minecraft was designed to allow other people to modify it. You can add mods that change gameplay and resource packs that change the look and feel, and you can play created maps that you download. However, it is very easy to download an application or file that can damage your game or your computer. We recommend that if you do want to modify your game, you enlist the help of a parent or a friend who has already successfully done this. You need to make sure that any new files or applications you use are compatible with the exact version of the game you are playing, make backups of your game files before making any changes, and check for viruses!

switch between modpacks. Each will give you a selection of different modpacks to play. There are hundreds of modpacks: some popular ones include Agrarian Skies, Attack of the B-Team, Crafting Dead, Crash Landing, Tekkit, several Feed the Beast pack variations, and TolkienCraft.

MODS

Mods (short for modifications) are programs you download that change something about the way the game operates. They may change gameplay, add more content (like new mobs or blocks), or make one or more tasks easier to accomplish. To use most of them you'll need to play a slightly older version of Minecraft, because it takes some time for mod creators to catch up with official game releases. It is easy to set up a profile with your Minecraft launcher application to use an older version. For many mods you will also need an application that helps load the

In the Twilight Forest mod created by Benimatic, an enchanted and forested new realm is added, populated by goblins, squirrels, fireflies, yetis, and much more, along with a progressive adventure that pits your wits against ever more dangerous enemies.

mod, called Forge. There are hundreds of excellent mods that are free of charge and created by talented Minecraft players and programmers. A few of the most popular mods are: Applied Energistics, BiblioCraft, Biomes O' Plenty, Carpenter's Blocks, Chisel, Ender IO, Extra Utilities, Forestry, Inventory Tweaks, JourneyMap, Lucky Block, Minefactory Reloaded, Mo' Creatures, OpenBlocks, Natura, NotEnoughItems, Optifine, Pixelmon, RailCraft, Thaumcraft, Thermal Expansion, Tinker's Construct, Waila, and WorldEdit. Be aware that different mods may conflict with each other, and as you add more mods, more computer memory is needed to run them. Many mods have both single-player and multiplayer server versions.

MULES

Like donkeys, mules are a type of horse, and behave similarly. Mules look like donkeys but have a darker coat. They can't wear armour, but they

Like donkeys, mules can have a chest and a saddle.

can carry a chest to help you transport stuff. Mules don't spawn naturally; you can only create them by breeding a horse with a donkey, but you can't breed two mules together.

On the Wynncraft multiplayer server (play.wynncraft.com) you take on a progressive series of adventure quests in a beautifully designed map, interacting with a variety of NPCs to complete your missions.

MULTIPLAYER

To play multiplayer, you will need access to a server or you will need a home network to set up your own server. If you are joining a server, you will need to understand the risks and requirements involved. It's best to have an experienced friend or parent show you the ropes for joining a server or setting up a server for you and your friends to play on. In multiplayer, you can chat with other players and form groups to build amazing cities, houses, and castles, or just survive together.

Some multiplayer servers are public servers where you play short mini-games. Other multiplayer servers let you play vanilla (unmodded) or modded Minecraft. Some popular multiplayer server styles, beyond playing Minecraft in non-PvP Survival or Creative mode, or mini-games, are Anarchy, which is PvP with almost no rules; Economy, which emphasizes shops and buying and selling; Factions, where you join a team and battle against others; and Prison, in which you work to reach higher levels in a prison setting.

The easiest way to set up a multiplayer world for playing vanilla Minecraft with a few friends is through Minecraft Realms. This is a Mojang service that lets you set up an online world and share it with other players, but it does require a monthly fee. Realms also has several built-in custom maps and mini-games that you can play.

MURDER HOLE

A murder hole is a 1x1 hole, usually situated at the level of a hostile mob's feet. It lets you attack

You can be quite safe killing mobs through a murder hole.

The Mushroom Island Biome is the only biome that doesn't spawn hostile mobs.

through the hole, protecting yourself, and then easily gather the drops when the mob dies. When you make a murder hole, you should be standing on the level below the hole. Making temporary barricades with murder holes is a great way to handle mobs when there are too many for you to fight or when you are at low health.

MUSHROOM ISLAND BIOME

The Mushroom Island Biome is extremely rare, and it's the only place you can find the mooshroom, a cow/mushroom hybrid that you can milk with a wooden bowl for mushroom stew. A mooshroom looks like a cow with a red mushroom skin and red mushrooms growing on its back. In fact, if you shear the mushrooms off a mooshroom's back, it will turn back into a regular cow. The mushroom biome also grows giant mushrooms, on a special dirt-like block called mycelium, which lets mushrooms grow in any light level. You can break a giant mushroom for a mushroom harvest. Not all of a giant mushroom's blocks drop mushrooms though. A giant mushroom block drops up to two mushrooms, but may drop none at all. Mushroom Island is also the only biome in which hostile mobs don't spawn.

NAME TAGS

Name tags allow you to add a name to a mob (except the Ender Dragon) or a villager. They are a rare item in Minecraft, because they can't be crafted. You must either trade for them with a villager or be lucky and find one in a chest or fish one up. Once you have a name tag, you use an anvil to rename the name tag. Then, with the renamed name tag in your hand, right-click on a mob or a villager. This gives the entity the name, which shows above its head.

Normally, right-clicking on a villager brings up the trading screen. To work around this, you can construct a temporary Nether portal and right-click the villager when you are in the portal. Or, if you are playing in Creative mode,

Name a mob "Dinnerbone" and they'll go upside down and stay that way until you rename them.

you can grab a villager spawn egg from your inventory/item selection screen, rename the egg with the anvil, and then spawn the villager with the named egg. If you are playing on a multi-player server, another player can right-click the villager to open the trading screen, and then you can right-click the villager with your name tag.

If you name a mob "Dinnerbone" or "Grumm" (two Mojang game developers' usernames), the mob will turn upside-down. If you name a sheep "jeb_" (another developer's username, which has an underscore at the end), the sheep will have multicoloured wool. Naming a rabbit "Toast" will change the rabbit's skin to look like the pet rabbit of one of the game developer's friends. Placing a name tag on a mob will stop it from ever despawning.

NAVIGATING

Knowing where you are in the world is a good habit. In addition to helping you find your way home, it can also help you find your way back to where you died, so you can recover your inventory items. The best way to keep track of your home and where you are at any time is to use Minecraft's location coordinates, which you find by opening the debug screen. To open the debug screen, press F3 (or on some laptops, Fn+F3. Fn is the Function key). You are looking for the XYZ and Facing numbers, which are near the bottom of the screen.

X, Y, and Z represent three coordinates on three different axes. With these coordinates, the center of the world is at 0, 0, 0. The x-coordinate shows where you are along an east-west line. Negative numbers on the x-axis show you are west of 0, 0. The z-coordinate shows where you are along a north-south line. Negative numbers on the z-axis show you are north of 0, 0. The y-coordinate shows the altitude (how high you are) from down in the mines to the sky. The lowest level in the Minecraft Overworld is 0, at the bottommost blocks of bedrock. The highest level you can build at is 255. Sea level is 63, and clouds are at Level 127.

The Facing entry shows you what direction you are facing – east, west, north or south. Make sure you have your home base coordinates noted down somewhere, so that when you get lost you can just open up the debug screen and look at your current x and z position, then figure out what direction you need to go to get back to your home coordinates.

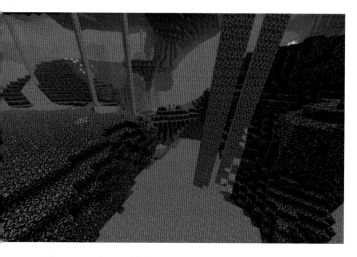

You'll see quite a bit better in the Nether with a potion of Night Vision, although you may not want to!

THE NETHER

If you want to make potions or if you want to defeat the Ender Dragon or Wither, you'll have to go to the Nether. While the Nether can seem scary, if you wear strong armour and have weapons, you can stay pretty safe. Zombie pigmen won't bother you if you don't attack them.

You can stop a ghast from firing at you if you get out of its sight. Wither skeletons and blazes spawn by Nether fortresses, and magma cubes are fairly rare and can't move as fast as you. You can use cobblestone, which is resistant to ghast fireball blasts, to build protected bridges and walls, to protect your portal, and to block off walls in a fortress until you are ready to explore. It is very easy to get lost in the Nether, and maps aren't much help. Make markers to show your path back to your portal, or make a screenshot of your coordinates in the debug screen. To make a screenshot press F2. If you get completely lost and you have obsidian, flint, and steel, you can create another portal to take you back to the Overworld. You can also make a chest, place your belongings in it, take screenshot of your x-, y-, and z-coordinates, and then jump into the lava to die! With coordinates in hand, you can return to your death site and grab your belongings from the chest.

NETHER FORTRESS

Your main priority in the Nether is to find a Nether fortress. Essential ingredients for any potion-making – Nether wart (growing at the bottom of

A Nether fortress can be a maze of similar corridors and rooms, so have a plan to find your way out.

stairs) and blaze rods for a brewing stand (dropped by blazes) are found in fortresses. However, it's difficult to see well in the dim light of a Nether fortress. A potion of Night Vision will make things brighter, or you can change your video settings to maximize the screen's brightness and the render distance. In the distance, a fortress will show up as a flat, tall, dark area. It has straight edges, compared to the rocky edges of netherrack cliffs and mountains.

You can make a Nether portal by placing lava source blocks in a frame and pouring water on them.

NETHER PORTALS

You can create a portal without needing a diamond pickaxe to mine obsidian. Instead, you make the obsidian by creating waterfalls against a wall, then pouring lava from a bucket into the blocks where the obsidian frame should be. You can also create frames out of non-flammable blocks like cobblestone to place lava blocks in and pour water over these.

When you create a portal in the Overworld, the Nether-side is created automatically. The Nether x- and z-coordinates are mapped with a 1:8 scale to the Overworld. One block in the Nether is equivalent to eight in the Overworld. When you make a portal in the Overworld, the Nether portal that is created is located at one-eighth of the x- and z-coordinates, and as close

to the Overworld y-coordinates as possible. What this means is that you can create networks of portals that make it easy to travel far distances in the Overworld. The most reliable way of doing this is creating the connected portals by hand. First you create the Overworld portal at coordinates x, y, and z. Travel to the Nether, and create a portal at the spot with the exact coordinates x/8 (the value of x divided by 8), y, and z/8. Match the y-coordinate as close as possible to the Overworld y. In the Nether, make railways or paths between your Nether portals.

OBSIDIAN

Obsidian is the toughest block in Minecraft except for bedrock (which you can't mine). Obsidian is required for building Nether portals and enchantment tables. You can find it in low levels, often by lava, and you'll need a diamond pickaxe to mine it. Obsidian is created when running water hits a lava source. (This means you can also create obsidian yourself, if you have a lava source and water, simply by pouring water over a lava source block.) When you find obsidian in a cave or mining, there is a good chance lava is nearby, even under one layer of obsidian. To protect yourself and stop mined obsidian blocks from falling into the lava, place water into a hole at the same level as the obsidian. When you break the obsidian, water will flow into its place, stopping lava from flowing there.

When you're mining obsidian, place water at the same level, so it can quench any lava that you uncover before the lava burns up the obsidian or you.

OCEAN BIOME

Ocean Biomes are made of water, as you would assume, going from ocean floor up to sea level at y=63. These biomes are often quite large, although you shouldn't find one any larger than three thousand blocks across. At shallower levels by mainland or by small islands you can actually find clay, so the ocean edge is an additional destination, beyond a river or a Mesa Biome, for finding this block. However, you should wear a helmet enchanted with Aqua Affinity (to increase underwater mining speed) and Respiration (to improve underwater breathing time and vision) and boots with Depth Strider (to improve your speed) for mining underwater. An Ocean Biome variation called Deep Ocean Biome is very similar to the Ocean Biome, except it can about fifteen blocks deeper than an Ocean Biome and is the home of ocean monuments.

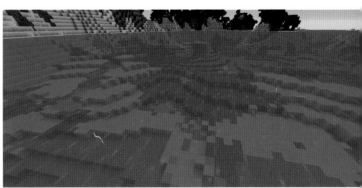

You can find clay at the bottom of the more shallow parts of the Ocean Biome.

OFF-HAND SLOT

Dual wielding – holding one item in each hand – is possible when using the off-hand slot. When you are already holding an item but want to use another, click F to equip the item in your off hand. This will let you do things like block and attack at the same time, choose the type of arrow you shoot with your bow, or light your way with a torch as you mine. The main hand takes priority over the off hand, but if the item in the main hand is unusable, the off hand slot will engage. You will not be able to attack with the off hand, however, even if the main hand is empty.

If you'd rather play left-handed, you can designate the right hand as the off-hand slot through a toggle in the skin customization settings. Mobs have dual wielding power as well, and while most mobs are righties, mobs have a 5 per cent chance of spawning left-handed.

PAINTINGS

When you place a painting on a wall, you'll randomly get one of twenty-six Minecraft paintings, in sizes 1x1 up to 4x4. The block where you place the painting will be the painting's bottom left corner.

You can create a secret passageway using paintings. First make your two-block-high, one-block-wide entrance. On one side of the two blocks that you'll be passing by, place a sign on each block. Then on the wall that you are concealing, right-click a painting on the bottom left block next to the entrance, until a painting comes up that covers the entranceway. The signs act like a full block, so a painting can be placed on them, but they also allow players to move through them as though they weren't there.

For a painting to cover an entranceway, place signs inside the entranceway.

PICK BLOCK KEY

Clicking the pick block key (usually a mouse's middle key) places the block your cursor is over into your hand, as long as you have that block in your hotbar. If you are in Creative mode, you don't have to have the block in your inventory at all to do this.

PIGS

To ride a pig, craft a carrot on a stick (a carrot with an undamaged fishing pole), place a saddle on your pig, and jump on. Pigs can also be led and bred with potatoes and beetroot. There is an achievement called When Pigs Fly. To accomplish this, you must ride the pig over a cliff

If you're riding a pig, it won't stop until you hold something besides the carrot on a stick, or until it has eaten the carrot. Other pigs will follow you, too.

so that the pig takes more than two hearts of fall damage. This means the fall needs to be about six blocks.

PILLAR JUMPING

Pillar jumping (also called pillaring up) is jumping and placing blocks beneath you. Pillar jumping is a great way to get out of a sticky situation, whether you need to get away from mobs or get out of a cave system. Listen for the sounds of lava or water if you are pillaring up and mining blocks out of

Pillaring up can help you get out of a ravine fast, as well as out of other sticky situations.

You'll only find villages in three biomes: Plains, Savanna, and Desert. Of the three, the Plains Biome is the only medium/lush biome, so the grass is greener and it will rain here.

Sunflowers only grow naturally in Sunflower Plains Biomes, and these two-block-high flowers always face east.

your way. You don't want to accidentally unleash either of them on top of you. You can also pillar down, which you would do if you were at the top of a cliff or large hole and wanted to get to the bot-tom. Drop sand (or gravel) until the pillar of sand is high enough for you to stand on, and then you can shovel your way back down.

PLAINS BIOME

Like Forest Biomes, Plains Biomes are fairly common. They are relatively flat and don't have many trees. This is the best biome to find horses in, although you can also find them in Savanna Biomes. Another reason to visit the Plains Biome is for the NPC villages you can find there.

A variation of the Plains Biome is the Sunflower Plains Biome, where you'll find hundreds of sunflowers, all facing east.

POISON

There are several ways to be poisoned in Minecraft. You can eat a spider eye, poisonous potato, or pufferfish, or be attacked by a cave spider or with a potion of Poison. You can tell you are poisoned because your health bar hearts turn a yellow-greenish colour. However, poison doesn't kill you; at most it will drop your health to one point (a half heart) and keep it there while the poison has effect. You can eat a golden apple to heal. Milk will also counter the effects of poison and harmful

Eating pufferfish will give you the Poison effect as well as the Nausea effect, which makes your screen distort.

potions, but it will also counter any effects from positive potions as well. If you eat rotten flesh, raw chicken, or pufferfish, you can get a similar effect called Hunger, which depletes your hunger bar. Eating pufferfish will also give you a Nausea effect that makes your screen distort and wave.

POTIONS

You use potions to give yourself or others special abilities or strengths, like Invisibility, or hindrances, like Weakness. These effects are often called status effects. To brew potions, you must have some ingredients you can only find in the Nether. A blaze rod, from a blaze, is needed to craft the brewing stand. Nether wart, which grows in Nether fortresses, is needed for making the base potion. To make potions of Regeneration, you'll need ghast tears; for Strength, you'll need blaze powder; and for Fire Resistance, you'll need magma cream from magma cubes.

Almost all potions start with making the base Awkward potion with water bottles and Nether wart. You then brew the results again, adding your main potion ingredient. This can be one of those listed above, or golden carrot for Night Vision, rabbit's foot for Leaping, sugar for Swiftness, pufferfish for Water Breathing, glistering melon for Healing, and spider eye for Poison. Once you've brewed this potion, you can usually brew it again with a modifying ingredient, either glowstone to make the effects stronger or redstone to make them last longer.

For some, you can brew with fermented spider eye to invert the potion. Night Vision potion will become Invisibility. Inverted Fire Resistance becomes Slowness, and Healing and Poison inverts to Harming. You make the potion of Weakness with just water and fermented spider eye. Finally, you can brew your potion with gunpowder to turn it into a splash potion, and add dragon's breath to a splash potion to make it a lingering potion. Don't throw potions of harm at the undead, like zombies or skeletons – this will only heal them. To damage them, throw potions of healing.

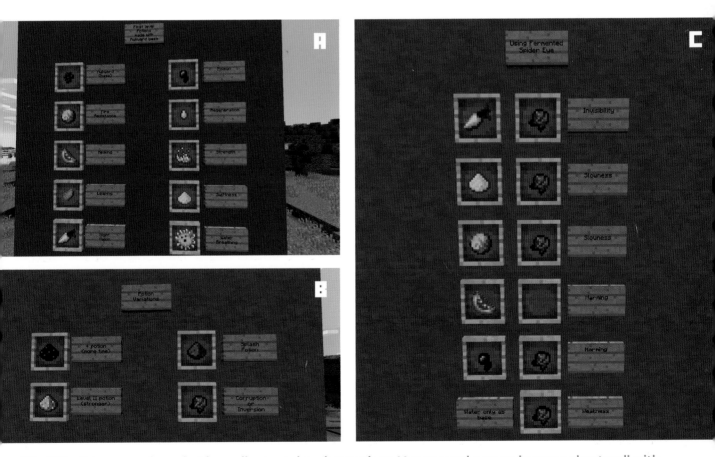

It's difficult to remember what ingredients make what potions. You can make up an in-game cheat wall with notes to help remember how to make first level potions (A), what ingredients modify the first level potions (B), and what fermented spider eye does when you add it to a first level potion to corrupt or invert it (C).

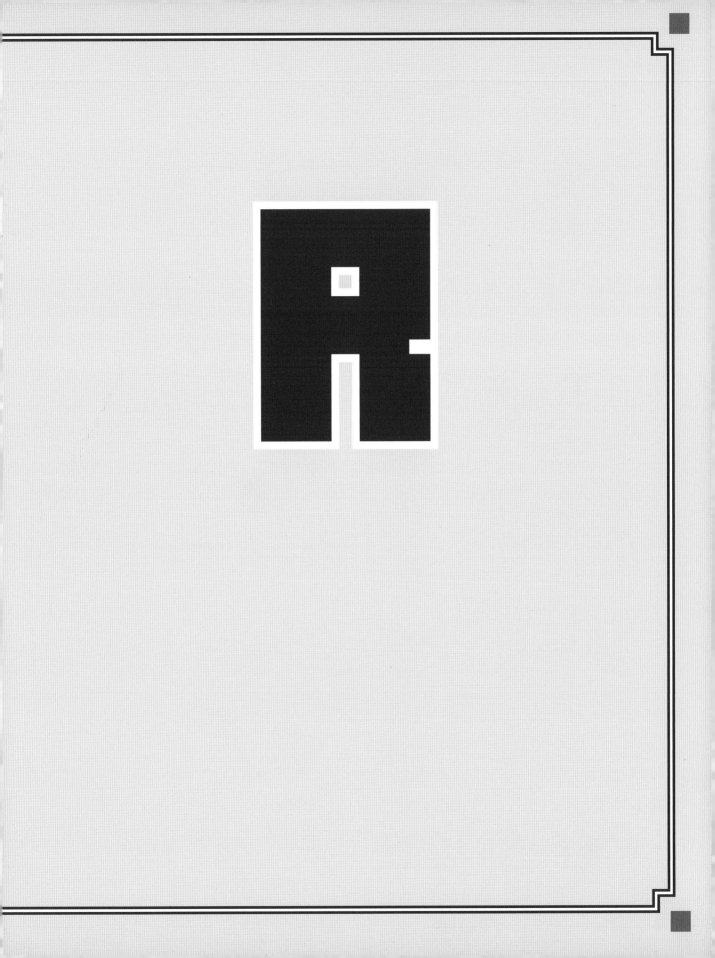

Glass in the block above the rail will stop zombie pigmen from spawning on or crossing rails in the Nether.

RAILS

Building railways with rails and powered rails can help you move quickly around the Minecraft world on a minecart. You can travel down to your mines, to villages and villagers, to visit another player, or to connecting portals in the Nether. The rails themselves are expensive though. You need six iron and a stick to craft sixteen minecart rails, and six gold, a stick, and redstone to craft six powered rails. It's helpful to find an abandoned mineshaft early in the game so you can loot them for their rails.

Remember that you're not safe from mobs on railways. The safest railways are either underground, in lit corridors that mobs can't spawn in, or elevated. If you are building an elevated railway, make sure to keep it lit and well away from trees and other blocks that mobs can jump from. For full speed for an occupied minecart on a level surface, place a powered rail every thirty-four blocks. Going uphill, place powered rails every other block. To keep your tracks clear of zombie pigmen in the Nether, place glass blocks (or other blocks that the game sees as transparent, like leaves or stairs) one block above the rail. You can move through these blocks without suffocating when you're traveling on a minecart, but the pigmen see them as an obstacle. The zombie pigmen won't spawn on the rails or move across them.

RAVINES

Ravines, like caves, can be good sources to find exposed ore. There are several ways to get down

Always look in a ravine to see if there is an abandoned mineshaft or stronghold exposed.

a ravine. Drop blocks of sand or dirt at the edge, letting them drop all the way down. Once the stack is up to your level, jump on and dig down (pillar down).

Another way to get to the bottom of a ravine quickly is to use a waterfall. Pour some water so it flows into the ravine. Make sure that there is a puddle of water at the bottom for you to land in. Then step into the waterfall and let it carry you down. You can also swim back up a waterfall. Finally, if you have the time, you can just make steps down the side of the ravine.

REPAIRING

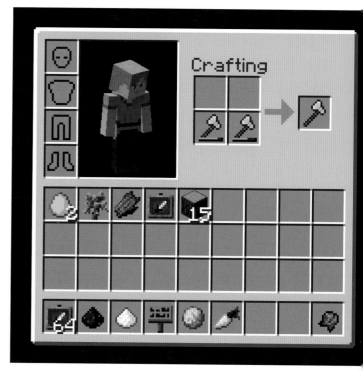

When you combine items to repair them, make sure there is at least 5 per cent damage between the two to get the bonus 5 per cent durability added.

It's a good idea to repair your weapons and tools before they break, especially during early game when your resources are low. Repair unenchanted weapons, tools, and armour in a crafting screen by combining two damaged items of the same type and material. If you make sure that the total damage between the two items is at least 5 per cent, the repaired item will get 5 per cent more durability than a freshly crafted tool. You don't have to get your calculator though to figure out the exact percentages for each tool. Just make sure that each tool's durability bar is a little down, more than a hair's width.

You can also repair tools and weapons with just their material using an anvil, but sometimes this costs more in materials than it would to just craft a new one. Repairing an item using the mending enchantment increases the item's durability by two for each XP orb. Whatever you do, don't repair an enchanted tool with a crafting screen. This will remove the enchantments. You'll need to use an anvil to repair any enchanted items.

You can change the way the game looks with resource packs like the John Smith Legacy JSC resource pack, developed by JimStoneCraft.

RESOURCE PACKS

Resource packs (or texture packs) are sets of files that replace game resources like sounds and textures (image files) that make blocks, water, and the sky look the way they do. They don't change the basic way the game plays. Some may make the world look more cartoony, others more medieval, and still others more modern.

As with mods, it can take a while for a resource pack creator to update their pack to match the latest Minecraft release, so to use a resource pack you may need to use a previous Minecraft version. With high resolution texture packs, you'll be using more computer memory as well. A resource pack is a zip file that you can place inside your applications "resourcepacks" folder. Once you've placed your resource pack files in this folder, start Minecraft, and under Options>Resource Packs you can load and unload the pack you want.

The dark oak trees in a Roofed Forest Biome are packed so closely together that it is very dark, and mobs spawn even during the day.

Popular resource packs include: Soartex/Invictus, DokuCraft, Faithful, John Smith, Sphax PureBDCraft, Modern, and Equanimity.

ROOFED FOREST BIOME

In a Roofed Forest Biome, you'll find dark oak trees and giant mushrooms as well as rose bushes and regular mushrooms. Because the canopy is so thick, you'll also find lots of hostile mobs.

You can find striking mountain landscapes in the Savanna M Biome.

SAVANNA BIOME

Savanna Biomes are one of the three biomes you'll find villages in, along with the Plains and Desert Biomes. Savanna is a dry biome, so it never rains here. Like the Plains, it is relatively flat and open, and horses will spawn here. Along with horses, you'll find the acacia tree, with its distinctive grey bark and orange wood, growing here. Variations of the Savanna Biome include the Savanna M Biome, which can have enormous mountains reaching very high in the sky past clouds. The Savanna Plateau Biome has flattened hills, or mountains, and the Savanna Plateau M Biome includes extreme cliffs at the edges of high, flattened hills.

SEEDS

When you create a new world in Minecraft, the game uses a random number called a seed to generate the world and its structures, like ocean monuments and villages. You can see your world's seed by typing /seed in the chat window. You can also enter your own number or sequence of characters in the more world options screen, under Seed for the World Generator. Lots of players look for great starting points or other notable features in new worlds and share the seeds for these online at websites like minecraft-seeds.net. If there's a world whose description you like, you can copy and paste or type that world's seed into your world options screen to start that world in your game. You do need to first make sure the world was created using the same game version you are using, and type the seed for that world into your world options screen.

You can type whatever you want in the Seed for the World Generator to use that code as the random number the program uses in generating the world, its terrain, and its structures.

SHIELD

Take advantage of dual-wielding power and craft a shield as soon as you are able to, using six planks and one iron ingot. You can customize the pattern on your shield by adding a banner. To use a shield, right click while you're being attacked. It will reduce damage taken and may knock back your attacker.

Using a shield will slow you to a sneaking pace, but it will block incoming attacks from creeper explosions, mob melee attacks, arrows, fireballs, and snowballs, among other things. When hit by an axe, the shield will be out of commission for five seconds.

SHULKER

After defeating the Ender Dragon for the first time and teleporting to an End city, beware of the shell lurker – shulker for short – hiding in its purpur-block-like shell. Shulkers pop up to peek shyly at you as you explore, but if you come within sixteen blocks, it will open up and shoot guided missiles which follow you as you attempt to escape. If a shulker leaves the comfort of a block or takes damage, it can teleport to safety. When its shell is closed, it has twenty armour points, so you'll need to hit it and collect the five XP when its shell is open.

If you attack one little silverfish, more will come, and that can add up to a lot of damage.

SILVERFISH

These small mobs hide in silverfish blocks (also called monster eggs) that look like stone or granite in Extreme Hill Biomes and in stronghold dungeons. There's no way to tell in advance if a block contains a silverfish.

If you break a silverfish block, you release a silverfish. It may come to attack you or settle in another block. If you attack a silverfish (and your strike doesn't kill it), the silverfish may call nearby silverfish out of their blocks to join in the fight against you, and a swarm of silverfish can do a lot of damage quickly. To stop a silverfish from calling reinforcements, you have to kill it without its death being recorded as your action. To do this, use a steel and flint to set the floor under the silverfish alight or drop a bucket of lava or blocks of gravel on it.

You can avoid any of this by paying attention to how long it takes each block to break – monster eggs take significantly longer to break with a pickaxe than their stone counterparts, so if it's taking a long time, you should stop. (Note, however, that if you are using your hand, it takes much less time to break a monster egg than it takes to break stone.)

Silverfish will suffocate if they are on soul sand.

SKELETON

When a skeleton (also called a skelly) attacks, it fires its arrows more rapidly the closer it gets to you. With the knockback of an arrow hit from a skeleton, you'll find it is difficult to get close enough to the skeleton to use a sword, and you can be hit and knocked back again and again. To avoid being hit, strafe (move sideways) by using your A key (to strafe left) and D key (to strafe right). Avoid knocking the skeleton back, as this gives it time to draw another bow and hit you.

Skeletons with armour or enchanted bows are even harder to kill; skeletons are more likely to spawn with armour or enchanted bows

Skeletons will run away from wolves, even if that means they have to run into sunlight.

during a full moon. Although the skeletons will usually burn in daylight, they will be unharmed if they are wearing a helmet. Sometimes the best option is to run away. If you get sixteen blocks away from a skeleton, they'll lose interest.

Skeletons are not solid, and they don't give you contact damage like zombies. If you are close to one, and its back is against a wall, step into the block it is standing in. You are now inside the skeleton and can kill it with your sword. The skeleton can't do anything. Keeping dogs (which are tamed wolves) nearby can also help defend you against skeletons. Wolves – tame or wild – will attack skellies immediately and skeletons will run away from them.

SKINS

You can change the way your player character looks by uploading an image file called a skin. There are two types of skin. The Steve skin has four-pixel-wide arms, and the Alex skin has a three-pixel-wide skin. In your Minecraft account you specify which one you are using, and you need to make sure that your skin is designed for either Steve or Alex. You can find skins online at websites like minecraftskins.com or create your own using a skin editor. You can also download a skin template for either four- or three-pixel arms at minecraft.net.

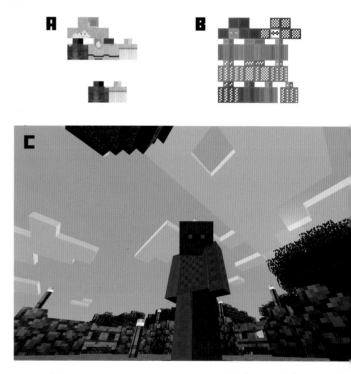

A skin file is an image file that has different locations for colouring different parts of the body. This is the Alex skin (A), the Alex skin template file (B), and what the template files looks like as a skin (C).

If you're mining below or around Level 40, and you hear the squelching sound of a slime, you have probably discovered a slime chunk.

Skins can have additional layers for your head, body, legs, and arms, which you can switch on and off independently in your Options>Skin Customization settings. The template that Minecraft provides helps show what part of the skin goes where. You can even choose to wear the template file as a skin to see what coloured area on the skin file belongs to which body type.

To assign a new skin file, log in to your account at minecraft.net and go to your profile page. Click Browse to locate the new file on your computer and then Upload to change your skin.

SLIME

Slimes are relatively rare. In swamps, slimes will only spawn at night where the light is at a level of seven or below. There's a greater chance of them spawning during a full moon. Slimes can also spawn in some chunks (about one in ten) at any light levels at altitude levels of forty or below. You can find online calculators that will take your world seed and tell you which chunks will spawn slimes. As with their Nether cousin the magma cube, kill the large ones first and then move on to the smaller ones.

SNOW GOLEMS

Snow golems are one of the two utility mobs along with iron golems. They will never spawn naturally; you have to make them from two snow blocks topped with a pumpkin. Snow golems can help defend you in your home or in battle by knocking back mobs with their snowballs. You have to protect snow golems against the rain, and you can't keep them in warm biomes like deserts, because they'll melt. Because they leave a trail of snow, you can use a snow golem for an infinite snow supply. Trap your snow golems on a wood or stone block with fences and a roof block. Then you can use a shovel to mine the corner of the block they are standing on to collect stacks and stacks of snowballs.

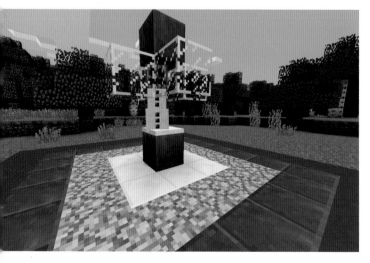

Capture (and protect) a snow golem, and you can get infinite snowballs from mining the corner of the block he's on.

SPIDERS

Spiders are neutral mobs because they are docile at daylight levels of light unless you attack them. However in the dark, at light levels of seven and below, spiders become hostile. You can always tell when a spider is nearby because of its hiss. If you can hear one but don't see it, check the tops of nearby trees and your roof.

If you are playing on Hard difficulty, spiders can sometimes spawn with their own status effect. Spiders in a Hard difficulty world can spawn with permanent (not potion-related) Invisibility, Regeneration, Strength, or Swiftness effects.

The best way to kill a spider is with a bow and arrow from a distance. If you are using a sword,

You can only see the red eyes of a spider that has spawned with Invisibility.

make sure you are on a higher block than the spider to stop it from jumping on top of you and causing more damage. Because a spider is two blocks wide, you can make a barricade with a murder hole to attack the spider through.

About one in one hundred spiders spawn with a skeleton riding on its back. This is called a spider jockey, and it is a very powerful combination with the strength of both mobs together. If you can't just avoid a spider jockey altogether, use a bow and arrow to try to kill the skeleton first and then the spider.

SPRINTING AND JUMPING

Running from a creeper or another player in PvP? If you sprint and jump at the same time, you'll go faster than if you are just sprinting. You'll move even faster if you sprint and jump in a two-block-high tunnel. For even greater speeds, make the two-block-high tunnel with ice blocks as the floor (packed ice won't melt with light) and trapdoors overhead. These ice tunnels can be a great alternative to railways for getting places fast.

In a 2x1 tunnel with packed ice at the bottom and trapdoors above, you'll move incredibly fast sprinting and jumping.

STATUS EFFECTS

Status effects are temporary abilities or impediments given to a mob or player. You'll hear positive status effects referred to also as *buffs* and hindrances as *debuffs*. In Minecraft, status effects are mostly given through food, potions, and beacons. There are twenty-seven status effects in total, although some aren't available through regular Survival gameplay, but instead only through custom commands. Status effects also give players and mobs a visual effect of curling particles rising around them; the colour of the particle depends on the effect. Status effects have levels, and the higher the level, the stronger the effect. If you drink a bucket of milk, you'll remove any status effect on you.

Potions can grant Absorption, Instant Damage, Instant Health, Invisibility, Jump Boost, Night Vision, Slowness, Speed, Strength, Water Breathing, Weakness, Luck, Bad Luck, and Poison. Beacons can grant Haste, Jump Boost, Regeneration, Resistance, Strength, and Speed. Eating pufferfish gives Nausea, Hunger, and Poison; golden apples give Absorption and Regeneration, and enchanted golden apples give Absorption, Regeneration, Resistance, and Fire Resistance. Rotten flesh, raw chicken, and pufferfish can also give Hunger. An elder guardian can give Mining Fatigue, and a sword enchanted with Bane of Arthopods gives spiders, cave spiders, silverfish, and endermites the Slowness effect. Status effects that are only available with commands are Blindness, Health Boost, and Saturation. Being hit by a spectral arrow causes Glowing, while being hit by a Shulker projectile causes Levitation. Status effects are displayed on the heads-up display (HUD), with positive effects on the top row and negative effects below.

STRONGHOLDS

Strongholds are the only place you can find the

Each status effect gives a player swirling particles in addition to the effect, with different colours for different effects. Strength produces a red particle.

End portal for traveling to the End. They are great structures to loot and fun to find, even if you don't care about getting to the End.

Each Minecraft world you create has a maximum of 128 strongholds. They are a maze of dungeon-like rooms that are generated somewhat randomly. (If you are digging through a wall, be careful – silverfish hide in many of the stone bricks of a stronghold.)

You'll find up to four chests in corridors, resting on stone slabs. These chests can contain a few of the following items: apples, bread, diamonds, enchanted books, Ender pearls, golden apples, iron horse armour, swords, pickaxes, armour, redstone, or saddles.

You may find one or two libraries, which may have one or two floors. On the first floor

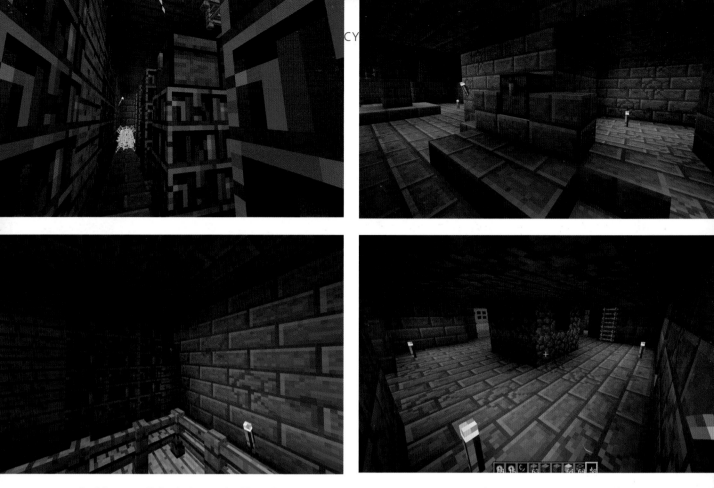

In strongholds, you'll find chests in libraries and along corridors. You'll also find them on the second floor of a storage room – climb the ladder to get there.

of a library is a chest at the top of a bookshelf. On a second floor (if there is a second floor), there's a chest in the corner. Library chests can contain a few items, such as books, enchanted books, paper, compasses, and unused maps.

A stronghold may also have one or more storage rooms. These are large square rooms with a well-like structure made of cobblestone in the centre. A ladder in the corner leads up to a second floor, where you will find another chest. These may contain a few of the following: apples, bread, coal, iron ingots, redstone, gold ingots, an enchanted book, or an iron pickaxe.

SUGAR CANE

You have to have sugar cane to make paper for books, for an enchanting table, and sugar for potions. It's also a great, easy resource to trade with villagers, because it is common during early trade and easy to grow. Sugar cane grows three blocks high on sand, grass, or dirt equally fast, but it needs to have at least one side of its land block touching water. One easy way to grow sugar cane is to plant rows, two blocks wide, into a pond, with a block of water to the left and right.

To harvest, break just the second block of the sugar cane. This makes both the second and third blocks fall, and leaves the bottom block ready to grow more. It's hard to see sugar cane if it pops off into the water or into the bottom block of cane. If you plant four rows, eight blocks long each, you'll have one full stack when you harvest, so you can easily tell if you've missed some. Or, if you are making trenches for the water between your sugar cane rows (instead of using existing pond water), you can place a single water source at one end of the trench. The water flowing down the trench will pick up any harvested sugar cane that falls into it and bring it to one end. There you can jump in the water to pick up the cane, or add a hopper connected to a chest for automatic collection.

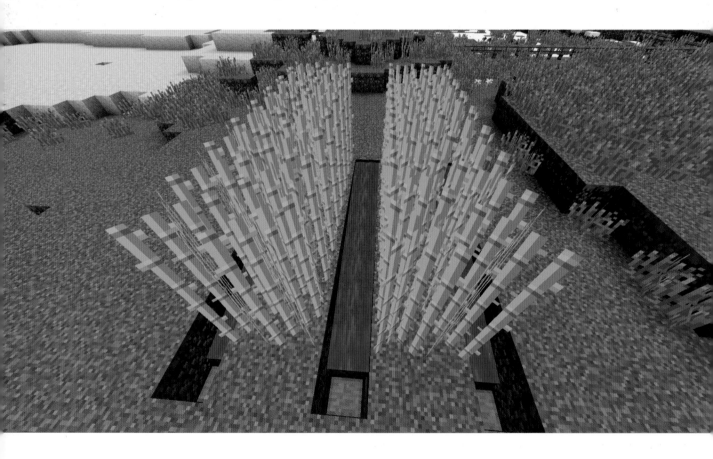

An easy sugar cane farm – four rows, eight blocks long, with water flows to collect cane that falls in the water and bring it to a hopper connected to a chest.

The Swampland Biome is the only biome that can have different temperatures in the same biome, so you can find different coloured leaves and grass right next to each other.

SWAMPLAND BIOME

The Swampland Biome is flat, greyish land with many shallow ponds. In the Swampland Biome you will find lily pads you can use to walk on water, slimes to kill for slime balls, vines to help make mossy cobble, and clay for bricks. You'll also find mushrooms, giant mushrooms, and witches' huts. The water, grass, and leaves here are darker than in other biomes. The Swampland Biome can have different temperatures within the same biome, so you can also see leaves and grass of different colours in the same biome. This is the only biome where oak trees grow with vines; unlike other biomes, these swamp oak canopies are all flat.

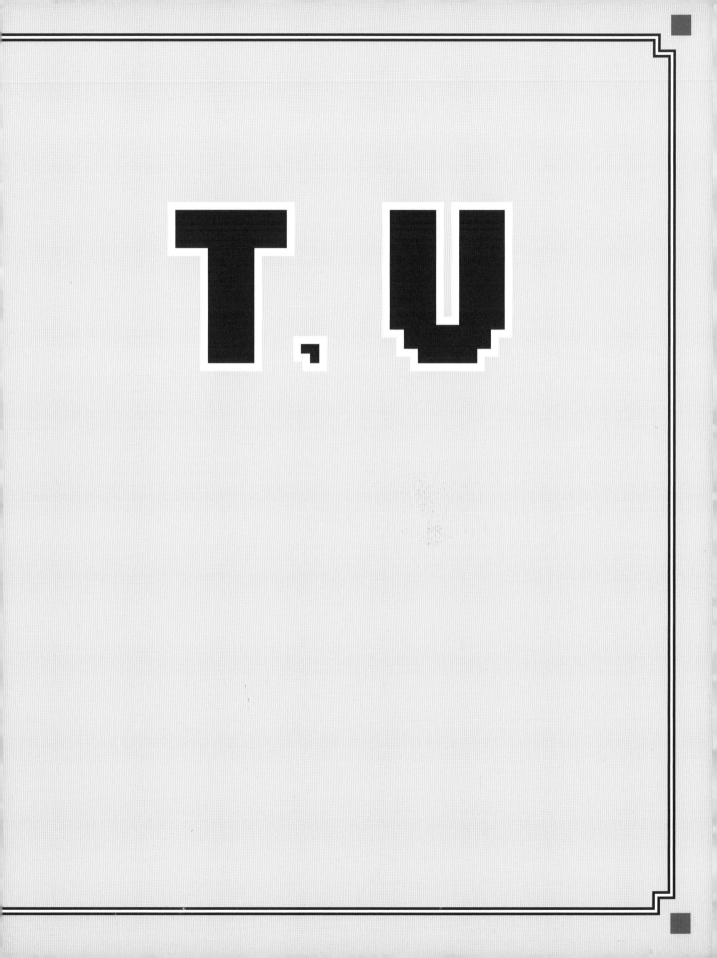

T, U

The sky flashes during thunderstorms – and it's the one time during daylight hours you can sleep.

TNT

You can craft TNT from sand (red or yellow) and gunpowder, and you'll also find it in desert temples. When you place your TNT, you prime it (or light it) by right-clicking with your flint and steel selected. You can also prime it with a redstone signal, from a redstone power source like a lever or button. TNT blocks flash several times before they detonate, giving you a warn-ing and enough time to get to safety. If you are using TNT to blast out a tunnel or large area or to level out a hill and you want a chain reac-tion, you'll need to place the TNT blocks close enough together to set each other off. This dis-tance varies with the type of block each TNT is surrounded by but is generally not much more than several blocks.

If the TNT for your chain reaction will be embedded in stone, you'll need to place the TNT blocks right next to each other.

TREES

Although there are only six tree species in Minecraft, each of these can grow in several shapes, with different heights, branches, and canopy shapes. If you're using a lot of wood, it's a good idea to start a tree farm so you don't clear your base area of trees. For an easy tree farm, grow saplings with four blocks of space between them. This gives them plenty of space for leaves to drop saplings. Leave a nine block space above the dirt where you plant the sapling, and then place a glass block or pane. This lets the light through but stops the tree from growing taller and making it difficult to harvest. Dark oak trees grow as four saplings together in a square – leave five blocks of space between each to get as many saplings from them as possible. You can also make your tree farm inside or underground. Saplings need a light level of nine to grow, so remember to light your farm.

VILLAGERS

When villagers were first introduced in Minecraft, they were called testificates (a made-up word). Villagers are a type of NPC (non-player character), and they spawn with villages. During the day, villagers walk around their village, going in and out of houses, and stopping to socialize with (or stare at) other villagers, mobs, and players. Villagers with brown robes will tend

Sometimes, for landscaping, you may want to force an extra-large oak tree with branches to grow from a sapling rather than one of the shorter oak tree shapes. To do this, place a ring of glass blocks around the sapling, a block above the ground.

to nearby crops, harvesting mature crops and planting seeds. When it's night time, or stormy, villagers rush inside. They tend to congregate together in a few specific houses in the village, usually nearer the centre. All villagers have a hidden inventory with eight slots, but they can only pick up wheat, wheat seeds, bread, carrots, and potatoes. Villagers with a lot of food sometimes share with other villagers.

You can breed villagers by making them willing to breed and making sure there are enough doors in the village. To make them willing to breed, they must have at least three bread loaves or twelve carrots or twelve potatoes in their inventory. You can throw them these supplies using the drop item key (Q on a PC).

Villagers will also only breed if there are enough doors in the village. The village population must be less than 35 per cent more than the total number of village doors. If your village is full, to add space for two new villagers, you'll need to add seven doors. You can add more doors to existing buildings or create new houses nearby. The only rule for doors is that, in the five block space in front of and behind the door, there must be more ceiling blocks behind than in front. A valid village door can be as simple as a door with one dirt block above and behind it. There must be at least two willing villagers near each other for them to breed. That will spawn a baby villager.

There are eleven types of jobs that villagers can have. Fishermen, shepherds, farmers, and fletchers (villagers who make bows and arrows) all wear brown farmer robes. Armourers, tool smiths, and weapon smiths all wear black blacksmith aprons. In white aprons are butchers and leatherworkers. Clerics are in purple robes, and librarians wear white robes.

VILLAGER TRADING

You can trade with villagers for hundreds of items, from melons, rotten flesh, and paper to diamond pickaxes and bottles o' enchanting. Emeralds are

If a village population is low, and two villagers are willing and near each other, they'll go into love mode. This produces hearts and a baby villager.

the main currency. Villagers will buy goods off you in exchange for emeralds. The types of trading offers that a villager will make you depend on that villager's job. For example, butchers buy and sell meat and fletchers buy string and sell bows. When you first trade with a villager, they'll give you just one trade offer. As you trade with them more, more of their trade options will unlock. Different villagers will have different prices for the same items, so it's a good idea to look for the villagers with the best trades. Villagers can also get tired of trading the same thing with you, and stop accepting a trade. You can make this trade unlock again by trading other items until they change their mind. When they will unlock an old trade is random. When a new trade is unlocked, you'll see green and purple particles over the villager's head.

VILLAGES

Villages are a great source for rare items in Minecraft. You can get carrots, wheat, and potatoes from village farms, trade with villagers, or find bookshelves in their libraries. If the village has a blacksmith's shop, there will be a chest there that might have armour, weapons, gold, diamonds, or other rare items in it. Villages can be found in the Desert, Plains, and Savanna Bi-

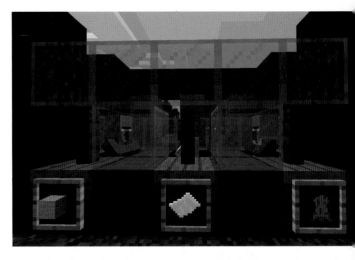

If you've found a villager with great deals, cordon them off and protect them so you can return for more of that trade. Remember baby zombies can get through one-block holes!

omes, although they are fairly rare. Villages are vulnerable to zombie sieges, which can wipe out their population.

To help a village survive, fence or wall it in, and create an iron golem or two if the village doesn't have one. If you don't have the supplies yet, you can protect villagers temporarily by placing blocks over the doors of houses they are in, to stop zombies getting at them. You can jail your villagers as long as you like, and they don't need to be able to get out. Light up the village and nearby areas, and remove or cover any pools of lava they could step in. Add blocks at the bottom of wells so they can climb out (ten sand for each of the four spaces will bring a well up to wading depth), and cut down any cactus

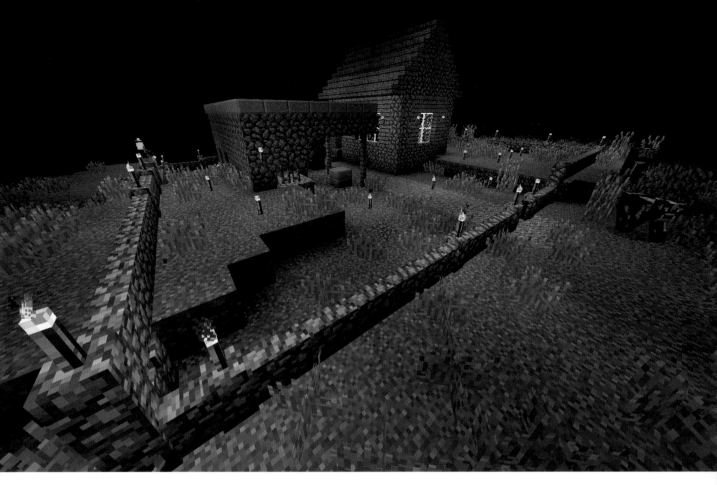

When you fence in a village, check it very carefully all the way around for blocks near the wall where a mob could jump to get in or out.

they could step on. If you're spending a lot of time near to a village, sleep through the night to stop night time mobs from spawning nearby.

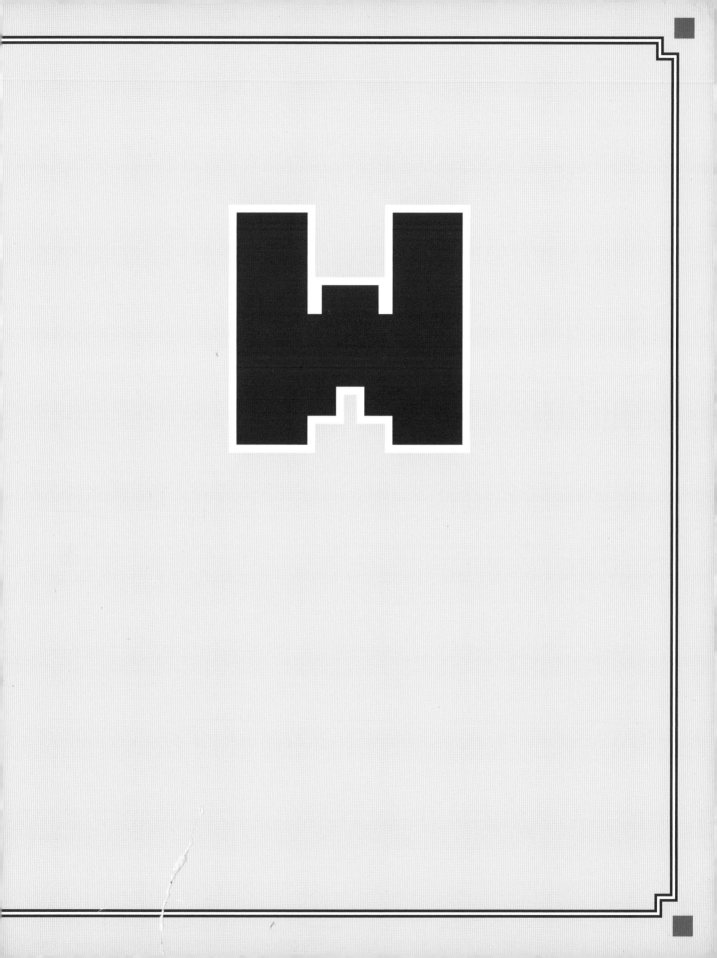

WATER

Wherever you place water, that block is called a water source block. On flat ground, a water source block will flow exactly seven more blocks in each of the four cardinal directions well as into the blocks in between these directions. The total length of the water flow along the cardinal directions is eight blocks of water. If you lower the ground at the final, eighth blocks, the path of water can keep flowing another eight blocks in each direction at that new lower level.

Water can be very useful, or destructive, in the way it forces some blocks to break and drop. Flowing water will break grass, flowers,

A fast way to fill a pond is to use ice blocks diagonally. Then work around the edges to add more source blocks where you find any flowing water.

torches, rails, cobwebs, and more, so you can use it to quickly clear an area of grass or a mineshaft of rails.

To make a never-ending supply of water, dig a 2x2 hole, one block deep. Place water in two corners opposite each other with water. This fills all four spaces with source block water that will replenish automatically. Now you can refill your bucket as many times as you need!

If you're creating a pond and you need to fill it with water, you'll want to fill one block level at a time to make sure that your pond is filled with static water, not flowing water. Flowing water makes noise, can trap and drown animals, and uses up more computer memory.

The fastest way to add water source blocks is to place water diagonally from corner to corner. If you can, use ice blocks (not packed ice) instead of water buckets and then break them with a pickaxe. Ice blocks are easy to transport, because you can stack them up to sixty-four. Each bucket of water takes three iron and one slot in your inventory, or you have to make many rounds between your water source and the pond. Once you've placed the water diagonally, you can work your way around the outside edge of the pond.

If you find a flowing water block, add water from your bucket or an ice block in that space. When you do this, the water you placed will usually fill up several flowing water blocks, so you don't have to fill every single flowing water block with a water source.

WITCHES

Witches look remarkably like Minecraft's peaceful villagers. However, they are one of the most harmful mobs you can encounter in the Overworld. They spawn in witch huts in swamps and in areas with light below seven. To attack you, they will use potions of Slowness, Poison, Weakness, and Harming. What makes them so powerful is their ability to heal and help themselves

When a witch drinks potions, its nose sticks out.

When you get a Wither to half strength, it lowers in the sky and is immune to arrows. Eat a golden apple or use a Regeneration potion, and run in with an enchanted sword to finish it off.

with potions. They'll use potions of Swiftness, Water Breathing, Fire Resistance, and Healing, and you'll see bubbles around them when they are drinking potions.

If you see them, your best bet is to stay sixteen blocks away and shoot them with a bow and arrow. If this isn't possible, sprint to the witch as fast as you can to stop it from getting a potion ready and kill it with your sword.

THE WITHER

The Wither is a boss mob that can only be created by a player. You build a Wither like an iron golem, but with soul sand in a T. Then you place three Wither skeleton skulls on the top of the T. When you place the last skull, the Wither is spawned immediately. As it gathers strength, it flashes, grows, and creates a large explosion that can be heard throughout your world. It

Wither skeletons drop the valuable Wither skull, and you need at least three Wither skulls to make a Wither.

rises into the sky, and will attack players and all mobs except the undead, like skeletons and zombies. It flies quickly and shoots powerful, explosive, black and blue Wither skeleton skulls. The black skulls are faster than the blue ones, but the blue ones can destroy any block but bedrock. When it attacks you it can give you the Wither effect, which gives a point of damage every two seconds for ten seconds.

You will need to use Healing and Strength potions on yourself as well as strongly enchanted diamond armour and weapons to defeat the Wither. It is much easier if you have friends to help. First use your bow and arrow. When the Wither is at half strength, it drops closer to the ground. It also gets immunity to bows at this stage. Drink a Strength potion and run in with your enchanted diamond sword to kill it.

You can make a baby wolf and other passive animals grow faster by feeding them their favourite food. Little green sparkles show up when you are doing this.

Withers drop the rare and valuable Nether star when you kill them, which you need to craft a beacon.

WITHER SKELETONS

Wither skeletons look like regular skeletons but they are dark grey, carry a sword, and are taller—two and a half blocks high instead of two. They only spawn in and around Nether fortresses, and when they hit you with their sword, they give you the Wither effect. This lasts ten seconds and gives one point of damage every two seconds. A good tactic with Wither skele-tons is to create a barricade or two-block-high space that they can't pass through. Because the Wither effect can kill you and Wither skeletons can move fast, try to kill a Wither skeleton from a distance with bow and arrow. Also, because they can't pass through two-block-high spaces, you can stop them from following you by putting blocks on fortress corridors.

WOLVES

Wolves are a neutral mob, like Endermen, that spawn in colder Forest and Taiga Biomes. If you attack them, they will attack back. They also at-

An amplified world type has a spectacular landscape but can be hard on computer memory.

tack skeletons, rabbits, and sheep. You can tame them by feeding them bones – this can take up to twelve bones. A tamed wolf has a collar, which you can dye to a different colour. Tamed wolves are also called dogs.

You can feed wolves to heal and breed them with any meat. You can also make a baby wolf grow up faster by feeding it meat. Wolves can also eat rotten flesh and raw chicken without getting poisoned.

To make a wolf sit, right-click the wolf. Right-click it again to release it. Tamed wolves will usually (but not always) teleport to you if you are more than twelve blocks away and they are not sitting. Times they don't teleport include when they are in a minecart or on a lead, or if you are in a different dimension (the Nether or the End). Tamed wolves will attack any mobs that damage you, except for creepers and your other pet wolves.

WORLD TYPE

When you start a new world in Minecraft, you can choose between several preset types of world or you can customize it. After you click Create

New World, click More World Options. You can cycle through your options by clicking the World Type button. Default will create a regular Minecraft world. You can choose a Superflat world with four layers (grass, two dirt layers, and bedrock) or choose a preset Superflat world like Snowy Kingdom or Redstone Ready.

You fully customize your world with the Customize button. This will allow you to select the sea level, turn on and off whether specific structures like temples and ocean monuments are included, decide how rare lava lakes should be, and more. If you make a Superflat world with only four layers, you'll have slime spawning because the entire world is below Level 40. To fix this, customize your Superflat world to be at least forty-one blocks deep.

Another world type you can create is a Large Biomes world. In this type of world, biomes will be about sixteen times larger. This can make it more difficult to find specific biomes, but may make your world feel more realistic. You can also choose an Amplified world. This makes the landscape extremely mountainous, but it can be hard on slower computers.

If you hit a zombie pigman by accident, you'll need to get at least thirty-two blocks away for a minute before the pigman horde forgive you and stop attacking. Often you have to travel even farther than this!

ZOMBIE PIGMEN

Zombie pigmen are neutral Nether mobs that spawn frequently in the Nether and in the Overworld by Nether portals. Zombie pigmen won't attack you unless you damage them, but if you do, they will call any nearby pigmen to chase and attack you. A pigman will keep attacking you until you get at least thirty-two blocks away from it and about forty seconds have passed. Some zombie pigmen spawn as baby zombie pigmen. They behave the same way as adult pigmen, except they are faster, like baby zombies. The best tactic with pigmen is to not damage them, and if you do accidentally, try to escape without damaging any more pigmen and get some distance away before you return to the Nether.

ZOMBIES

Zombies are the most common hostile mob in Minecraft. They are slow, so unless you are al-

Use a potion of Weakness and a golden apple to cure a zombie villager or baby zombie villager.

Zombie sieges of around twenty attacking zombies are real in-game events in Normal and Hard difficulty. You can't protect a village from a siege by lighting it or fencing it in. There's a 10 per cent chance every night that a siege will happen to one of your world's villages. A siege will only happen at or after midnight, when a player is near a village centre and if the village has at least twenty villagers. None of the zombies spawned for a siege are villager zombies.

ready damaged or cornered by a mob, zombies are easy to defeat. You can't mistake their groans as they approach, and if it's daytime, you don't even need to fight – all you have to do is have the zombie chase you into sunlight. As long as it doesn't have a protective helmet on, the sunlight will destroy the zombie. When you do attack zombies directly, they can sometimes call other zombies nearby to help them fight you. This happens more often in Hard difficulty. Zombies can also turn villagers into zombie villagers, and villager babies into baby zombie villagers.

ZOMBIE VILLAGER

A villager that has been attacked by a zombie has a chance of turning into a zombie villager. In addition, 5 per cent of zombies spawn as zombie villagers naturally. You can cure zombie villagers and turn them into regular villagers with a little effort. First, isolate them in a chamber with a roof. This stops them from killing other villagers and from burning in the sun. Then splash them with a potion of Weakness and feed them a regular golden apple. If this is successful, they'll make a loud sizzling sound and start shaking. After a few minutes, they'll turn back into a regular villager.